ROSES MADE EASY

COMPLETE GARDENER'S LIBRARY™

ROSES MADE EASY

Paul
Peterson

National Home
Gardening Club
Minnetonka, Minnesota

Roses Made Easy

Printed in 2006.

Tom Carpenter
Creative Director

Julie Cisler
Book Design & Production

Michele Stockham
Senior Book Development Coordinator

Gina Germ
Photo Editor

Natalia K. Hamill
Mary Harrison
Maggie Oster
Barbara Pleasant
Contributing Authors

Justin Hancock
Molly Rose Teuke
Copy Editors

ISBN 1-58159-128-4
3 4 5 6 7 / 10 09 08 07 06
© 2001 National Home Gardening Club

National Home Gardening Club
12301 Whitewater Drive
Minnetonka, Minnesota 55343
www.gardeningclub.com

Photo Credits

William D. Adams: 28 (inset), 30 (2), 31, 33, 40 (2), 109, 114 (2); Jim Block: 22, 64; David Cavagnaro: vi, 55, 120, 121, 124-125; Walter Chandoha: 11 (3), 63 (2), 75 (2), 77, 81, 102, 112, 120, 142; Rosalind Creasy: 12, 60 (2), 61, 63, 78, 79, 101; Thomas Eltzroth: 14, 57, 65 (2), 67, 108, 138, 142; Derek Fell: 2-3, 6, 7 all, 8 (3), 9, 11, 12 (2), 13, 14 (3), 15, 18, 19, 21, 23, 26, 27, 28-29, 30, 31(2), 32 all, 34 (3), 35, 36 (2), 37 all, 38 (2), 39 all, 41, 42, 43, 45, 50 (3), 51 (5), 54, 55, 58 both, 59 (2), 62 both, 64, 68 both, 69 (2), 70 (2), 71, 72 (2), 75 (2), 77, 80, 81, 83, 84 (3), 85 (5), 94, 108, 109, 114, 126 (2), 127, 129, 133, 138, 149; Sally Ferguson: 49 all; Marge Garfield: 6, 10, 28 (inset), 69, 75, 138, 140 (2); Goodman/J&P: 26; Saxon Holt: cover, vii, 5 all, 10, 13 (2), 14, 15, 24 both, 25, 28 (inset), 30, 41, 43, 44, 46 all, 47 all, 48 both, 64 (2), 67, 73 (2), 76, 78, 110, 111, 118 both, 119, 126, 129, 135; Bill Johnson: 15, 23, 28 (inset), 34 (2), 36 (2), 38, 41 (2), 42 (2), 43, 44 (3), 45, 63, 65, 71, 73, 83, 130, 131, 133, 134 all, 142 (2); Chuck Kidd: 10; Michael Landis: 4, 6, 13, 40 (2), 51, 56, 60, 72; Maggie Oster: viii, 8, 14, 16-17, 33 (2), 35 (2), 38, 42, 43 (2), 45 (2), 50, 69, 70, 77; Hugh Palmer: 52-53, 55, 57, 59, 61, 74, 85, 86-87, 136-137; Jerry Pavia: 56, 57 (3), 61, 65 (3), 66, 67, 71 (2), 72, 73, 74, 79, 81, 84 (2), 103, 108, 110, 111, 135, 138 (3), 139 all, 140 (3), 141 all, 142 (6), 143 all, 148; Paul Peterson: 4, 15, 27, 144, 145, 146; Diane Pratt: 29 (inset), 51, 110; Stephen Swinburne: 11, 82 both; Mark Turner: 25, 28 (inset), 83, 115, 122, 128, 132; Weeks Roses: 26.

Illustrations

K&K Studios: 31, 99, 106 all, 107, 109, 110, 111, 115; Nancy Wirsig McClure, Hand to Mouse Arts: 7, 20, 88, 89 all, 94, 95, 96, 97, 98. 99, 100, 104 both, 105 both, 109 (2), 110, 119, 120, 121, 122, 123, 132; Deborah Moloshok: 56, 79, 115, 116, 117 both.

Contents

THE NEWS FROM ROSELAWN

The composer J. S. Bach once told a student that playing music is easy: "Just play the right note, at the right time, in the right way." Well, I say that growing roses can be easy too: "Just plant the right rose, in the right place, in the right way—that's all!"

Old Bach liked inspiring people to enjoy what he loved. I do too—I want to inspire you to grow and enjoy more roses. I love lots of plants—hot peppers, raspberries, lilies, beets, herbs—but roses are special. No other plant is so widely grown, so widely loved and so symbolic of what flowers mean to us in our daily lives.

It seems that every rose I grow has a personal meaning. I remember digging holes with my son in the rain to rescue four struggling plants of 'White Dawn', an impromptu gift from neighbors ... how the scent of 'Blanc Double de Coubert' reminds me of my grandma's dusting powder ... planting red *Rosa rugosa* in memory of an old friend ... and cutting huge, fragrant blooms of 'Mme. Isaac Pereire' for my sweetheart.

For a home gardener, I guess I've grown a fair number of roses (close to 100). They perform well for me with no special bother, maybe because I've tried to choose the right roses so I don't have to baby them. If neighbors stop by to admire them, I cut a bloom for them. Roses are to share!

Speaking of which, I'm going to share a few things I believe about growing roses.

Anyone can grow roses and enjoy them. If I can, you can! I'm really pretty lazy about my roses, once they're planted properly.

Perhaps no other plant is as widely misunderstood as roses. They don't have to be fussy growers or always get black spot. If you choose the right plants and grow them right, you can minimize the fuss.

You don't have to be rich or stuffy to grow roses successfully. You don't have to enter shows or belong to a rose society, although if you do you'll be with avid and dedicated rose growers from all walks of life.

You don't have to know Latin or French or German. (But it's fun to know a few terms to help you understand what you're growing.)

I don't believe in starting a chemical shootout with Mother Nature. With some roses, certain chemicals play a role, but I'm not going to be a slave to costly arsenals of heavy treatments to keep fussy plants alive when they don't belong where they're growing. I don't have time for it, and it's a vicious cycle anyway.

I didn't take to roses the way Bach took to music. About 12 years ago, I moved into an 1880s house called Roselawn. The grounds were wild and overgrown, but I had to recapture the flavor of that romantic, rose-crazy era. Lots of people, Master Gardener training, and trial and error have taught me a great deal.

Roses are forgiving. If you make a mistake, you can change things. You can always replace them with something new or rearrange them in your garden scheme.

And what choices we have! So much has changed in the rose world over the last 20 years or so. We home gardeners have a boggling number of roses to choose from—nearly 10,000 cultivars are available for purchase in the United States alone!

One thing I've learned from gardening is to ask other people what works for them. I've asked several rose gardening colleagues who are professional writers to contribute their experience and expertise. They've assisted me in creating a fresh, authoritative and well-rounded "new look" at roses for you, the members of the National Home Gardening Club.

We're going to help you select the right roses, understand their special features and growing requirements, and prepare the best home for them. After all, if you're building a house, you don't start by finding a good repairman. You do everything you can to build it right in the first place. The same holds true for growing roses.

Roses are a symphony of colors, scents, forms and rewards. I'll be your willing guide on our excursion through this rosy world. Enjoy roses—they're easy!

Paul Peterson

– Paul Peterson

❧ CHAPTER 1 ❧

THE LURE AND LORE OF ROSES

Where Would We Be Without Roses?

It's your sweetheart's birthday, your daughter's wedding, Valentine's Day, your parents' anniversary. What gift do you think of as a special expression of love or esteem?

Recall trying to mend a lovers' spat, and how you needed the perfect ice-breaker? Or how about that special day when you got engaged: what acted as the best possible messenger of all those feelings, of that unique time? What can convey how you feel, sometimes even better than words? Roses.

What would you choose to plant at the gravesite of a loved one? Possibly a fine tree, to symbolize immortality. But you'd do well to plant a rose bush. Why? Because the right plant would continue to grow there with little care, and it would give forth its timeless, sweet-scented blossoms to fill the healing breezes with their perfume.

You're tired of high-maintenance yards and need some versatile, hardy plants, you're moving to a new home, or you're building your dream vacation cottage. What plants provide the backbone for any landscape plans, almost anywhere in North America? Roses, of course. A better landscape plant would be hard to find.

Roses permeate our lives and our culture. They're rich in history, and in literary and romantic symbolism. They have a long and influential history in both Western and Eastern cultures, and may be the most universally grown and best-loved flowering plant on our planet.

ROSES REVEALED

Roses can give us lifelong enjoyment.

Portland, Oregon, is the "Rose City"—complete with a Rose Queen and her court—but roses will grow in every town in the United States.

star hotel with thousands of rose petals each week—to be strewn all over the bed in the honeymoon suite. Roses can be so much fun that it's no wonder we take rose growing seriously!

Gardening Freedom

The great thing about gardening is that anyone can do it. It doesn't matter what your gender, race, creed, political beliefs, education level, economic status or dexterity levels are—you can enjoy gardening. Blind and disabled people can garden. You can garden early and late in life and all the years in between, and you can garden early and late in the day and all the hours in between.

Officially, the rose is a member of the genus *Rosa* in the family *Rosaceae*. The genus has some 200 species and thousands upon thousands of cultivars ("cultivated varieties") and hybrids. Roses are related to raspberries (they share canes and thorns), apples, almonds, peaches and strawberries. Peter Beale, author of the encyclopedic *Roses*, speculates that roses have been cultivated in gardens for "only" 5,000 years.

Roses grow in the Arctic Circle and near the equator. It's hard to get any more adaptable than that. Oddly, no rose originates from the southern hemisphere.

Roses commemorate the happiest and saddest moments of our families, friends and ourselves. We grow them for our bouquets. We live immersed in their historical tradition. And once hooked, we want to grow more and more of them.

We enjoy roses in our romantic life. We give them to loved ones all the time. I know of a florist who supplies a four-

 TIP **ONLY THE ROSES**

What other flowering plants but roses have a special name for the people who devote themselves to growing them? We have the term "rosarian" for such people, but have you ever heard of a "zinniarian" or a "marigoldarian"?

Weddings and roses—a good marriage.

Cut roses brighten up our homes. Here, English roses mix with Old Roses.

You can set your own style and make your own mistakes. Plants and gardens are forgiving. They let you be yourself and experiment. If you make a mistake, nature (and the garden industry) always will provide a way for you to try again.

A Most Versatile Family

For centuries now, explorers, pioneers and plant hunters have found and brought back

TIP Don't be afraid of those Latin or French names used in gardening. You don't have to pronounce them from a lectern in front of 3,000 linguists; all you need to do is grow and enjoy them. As Shakespeare said,

"What's in a name? that which we call a rose
By any other name would smell as sweet."

wondrous "wild" roses from almost all corners of the globe. From the Mediterranean came the *Rosa moschata*, one of the important progenitors. A rambling Musk rose, most likely from Asia Minor, gave us countless rich-scented roses. From China came the *Rosa chinensis* with a climbing habit, itself the result of centuries of genetic selection and manual breeding. The Damasks were grown by the Greeks and Romans; they probably originated in the Middle East (hence the name, after "Damascus").

Horticultural research is ever seeking better ways to grow things, and lately the good folks in our land-grant universities

BEYOND HYBRID TEA ROSES

Some people view rose gardeners in a short-sighted way. They see us as living in a rarefied society of blue-ribbon show roses, with an attitude that's exclusive, stodgy and outdated (kind of a "Hybrid Tea Party"). That kind of gardening may be fine for some people, but it's not our style in this book!

Show roses have a well-deserved place, but the truth is that almost everyone can grow and enjoy roses. Roses aren't just for the rich. And rose shows can be fun! We'll show you how anyone can grow roses, regardless of budget. And we'll explore the wondrous array of new and rediscovered roses for home gardens and landscapes, and why we now have so many good roses to grow and enjoy.

and at our county extension services have realized that the home gardener needs good, up-to-date and understandable information too. Rose growers both new and experienced are rightfully concerned with responsible pest control and maintenance practices. So later on, we'll go into ways to deal with pests and diseases by using what the companies and colleges—and other home gardeners—have found to be effective.

Roses are used more and more in the home landscape.

Shrub roses can give a naturalized country-garden look.

ROSES THROUGH THE AGES

What's more romantic than a red, red rose? Shown—the Hybrid Tea 'Olympiad'.

The rose looks fair, but fairer we
it deem,
For that sweet odor which doth
in it live.
    William Shakespeare, 1609

It was roses, roses all the way.
    Robert Browning, 19th century

Roses in War
I sometimes think that never blows
so red
The rose as where some buried
Caesar bled.
    *Edward Fitzgerald, 1857
(translation of the* Rubaiyat of
Omar Khayyam, *ca. 1100)*

The very first recorded literary reference to roses is related to battle. In Homer's *Iliad*, written almost 3,000 years ago, the goddess Aphrodite uses rose oil to treat Hector after he has fallen in battle.

One famous rose symbolizes peace grown out of a long, long war. You can still grow the historic rose 'York and Lancaster', *Rosa x damascena versicolor*, a mottled white and red striped flower that gets its popular name from the warring English houses of Lancaster and York. Their forces wore the colors into battle in the Wars of the Roses from 1455 to 1485. Richard Plantagenet chose the white rose as the House of York's battle emblem; the Earl of Somerset countered with the red rose for Lancaster's banner.

While Napoleon was busy conquering Europe and Northern Africa, his empress, Josephine, gathered the spoils of conquest in the form of new rose plants for her vast gardens at la Malmaison. It is said that the protocols of war protected the roses on any captured French ship—no matter what,

Roses come in many sizes and colors. This is the Miniature 'Rise 'n' Shine'.

the plants were sent through to Josephine. Her roses were captured on canvas by Pierre-Joseph Redouté, the prints of whose original works still reflect the glory of those days

'York and Lancaster' has been cultivated for more than 450 years.

Roses as battle standards: For 30 years during the Wars of the Roses, the White Rose led York into battle against Lancaster's forces, who flew the Red Rose.

ROSES IN ART: THE VICTORIAN IDEAL

"Perhaps few people have ever asked themselves why they admire a rose so much more than all other flowers. If they consider, they will find, first, that red is, in a delicately graduated state, the loveliest of all pure colors; and secondly, that in the rose there is no shadow, except which is composed of color. All its shadows are fuller in color than its lights, owing to the translucency and reflective power of its leaves."

—John Ruskin: *Modern Painters*, v, 1860

and teach us what our predecessors grew.

Roses in Legend and Religion

Gather ye rosebuds while ye may,
Old Time is still a-flying.
Robert Herrick, 17th century

Time brings roses.
Portuguese proverb

Tales abound of enchantments and superstitions surrounding roses. In rural parts of England not so long ago, roses were often used to help a woman choose her mate. For example, on St. George's Day,

April 23 (which also happens to be Shakespeare's birthday), a girl would wear a red rose; if she dreamed of red roses she would have good luck in love.

On Midsummer's Eve in Somerset, England, it is said that a maiden should enter the churchyard and scatter rose petals in the light of the moon. At midnight she recites a verse and her lover's apparition appears to her. In some places it's considered unlucky to take a rose worn on the body and scatter the petals.

Cosmetics, the Church and the Rosary

Oh, my love's like a red, red rose,
that's newly sprung in June.
Robert Burns, 1794

Many colorful stories ponder the source of the rosary used in Christian prayer. Apparently the name, symbol and associated set of prayers evolved from a variety of Christian—or pagan—traditions.

For centuries, from the glory of Persia through the Roman Empire to the Middle Ages and today, roses have stood for luxury, beauty and sensuality. The Greek poet Sappho dubbed the rose "queen of flowers." Rose water, syrups, strewn petals, attar of roses, rouge—all have been used as adornments of the body, cosmetic enhancements on the

The full blossoms of deep pink 'Miss All-American Beauty'.

secular side of things. Cloistered ladies even wove rose petals into garlands to please their suitors. These romantic rose garlands bear a strong resemblance to prayer beads.

"Austrian Copper," R. foetida bicolor, really comes from Asia.

Species roses are simple, elegant and fragrant. This is Rosa rugosa alba.

Magenta-colored roses add hot hues to any garden.

Let us crown ourselves with rose-buds, before they be withered.
        Bible (Solomon 2:8)

Did the stern early Church usurp these practices and, as it did with the pagan celebration of Saturnalia, make them into Christian ones? It's entirely possible. At any rate, the rose was an early biblical symbol of the Virgin Mary. And Ecclesiasticus contains the reference, "like a rose planted on the rivers I have borne fruit."

Mary is also depicted as one who provides mankind a path to reclaim Paradise (a word derived from the Persian expression for "garden"). Paintings from the Middle Ages portray Mary in an enclosed garden to symbolize this

connection. The enclosed garden gradually came to be portrayed as an enclosure of roses, or a garland of roses, surrounding the Virgin Mary.

In the 11th and 12th centuries, collections of prayers in honor of the Virgin Mary were given such titles as "Our Lady's Rose Garden," "The Garden of Roses" and "Rosarium." Indeed, the word "rosary" is from the Latin, meaning a rose garden. Up to the 20th century, "rosary" was widely used as a synonym for any rose garden. Some historians note that the reference to the garden also comments on the similarity of the work of a gardener in the fields to the monastic life of prayer and service.

Gradually these collections of prayers were remembered by means of counting beads, and thus began the use of the rosary as we know it today. The word "bead" derives from the Saxon word, "bidden," and the Old English "bed" or "bede," which meant prayer. When one said one's prayers, one was "bidding the bede." Over the course of time, "bead" came to mean the small, round objects that were threaded together for use in the rosary.

In the 11th century Lady Godiva, better known for her naked horseback ride, showed a different side of herself when she

The light pink Grandiflora 'Queen Elizabeth' came out in 1954 to commemorate Britain's new sovereign.

directed "a circle of threaded jewels upon which she was wont to number her prayers to be hung about the neck of the Blessed Virgin's image in the church at Coventry," according to one William of Malmesbury.

The prayers of the rosary initially were varied. A more standardized set of prayers issued from the legend of Mary's appearing to St. Dominic during the Crusades, at which time

Copper-colored tones come from Rosa foetida.

One of the ancestors of 'Tropicana' was 'Peace'.

WHEN IS A ROSE NOT A ROSE?

Many garden plants bear the name "rose" in some form, yet aren't in the rose family at all. I guess people want roses year around, or something to remind them of roses, so they've given them names that reflect that sentiment (or should it be scentiment?).

Here are some plants that use "rose" in their names but belong to other plant families. Good plants all, and still as sweet by any name, but alas, they can only be rose "wannabes."

Common name	**Botanical name and description**
Christmas rose	*Helleborus niger* (buttercup perennials in the poisonous hellebore family, with rose-shaped, pink-and-white blooms that come on late in the year)
Lenten rose	*Helleborus orientalis* (similar to above but with cream-brown blooms in early spring)
Moss rose	*Portulaca grandiflora* (common annual with succulent ferny foliage and a variety of colors, including rose tones)
Rose of Sharon	*Hibiscus syriacus* (hardy, tall shrub with flowers of pink, white, red or purple tones, also known as althea) or *Hypericum calycinum* (foot-high groundcover, also known as creeping St. John's wort)
Rose mallow	*Hibiscus moscheutos*
Rose acacia	*Robinia hispida*, also known as bristly locust or moss locust (rose-colored flowers)
Rose-apple	*Syzygium jambos* (*Eugenia jambos*) (hardy deciduous prickly shrub)
Rosebay	*Rhododendron maximum* (hardy evergreen shrub or tree with clusters of rose-pink flowers, also known as great laurel); also, *Nerium oleander* (oleander, from the pink color of the flowers)
Rose campion	*Lychnis coronaria* (perennial with magenta-red flowers, also known as mullein pink)
Rose geranium	*Pelargonium graveolens* (tender garden geranium and common houseplant with purplish pink flowers)
Rose milkweed	*Asclepias tuberosa*
Rose-of-China	*Hibiscus rosa-sinensis*
Rose of Heaven	*Lychnis coeli-rosa* (annual with pink, red or purplish blue flowers)
Rose-of-Jericho	*Anastatica heirochuntica*
Rose pogonia	*Pogonia ophioglossoides* (an orchid with rose to white flowers)
Rosy milfoil	*Achillea millefolium roseum*

she gave him the prayers of the rosary said today. This set of prayers was spread by Dominican monks throughout Christianity. During the 13th and 14th centuries, the prayers and the growing popularity of prayer beads led to widespread use of the rosary.

One story which closely aligns the rosary with roses is that of Saint Theresa of Avila, who is said to have worn a rosary made from beads formed from dried rose petals. The sweet rose fragrance of her rosary followed her as she moved about the convent.

Whether the rose's spirit is borne in the sacred or the secular, surely that's a fetching thought.

Shakespeare wrote of the Eglantine or Sweetbriar, R. eglanteria.

SUB ROSA: A MEETING WITH HISTORY

In Roman times, senators would suspend a rose from the ceiling during a secret political meeting. The symbol signified that whatever was discussed "sub rosa"—under the rose—was to remain secret. The Latin phrase remains in our language today to mean "privately" or "confidentially."

THE ROSE IN AMERICA

For centuries, rose arbors have invited visitors into American gardens.

We want bread and roses too.
*Slogan of women strikers in
Lawrence, Massachusetts, 1912*

The rose is the national flower of the United States as formally proclaimed by the White House and Congress, as well as popularly proclaimed by gardeners. In the U.S. we practice a "national rose consciousness." If you grow roses in Texas, you can talk to a rose gardener from Maine,

Gathering rose petals in the historic rose gardens of Old Sturbridge Village, Massachusetts.

Muncie or Marin County about the climate, the challenges and the rewards.

Tom Christopher in his *In Search of Lost Roses* (Summit Books, 1989) says that the Indians of the James River Valley were growing roses when Captain John Smith arrived. William Penn came to America with rose plants in 1699; Thomas Jefferson planted the white-blossomed climbing "Macartney Rose" a century later at Monticello. The first rose class developed in the U.S. was the Noisette, a cross between the Musk and the China rose made by John Champney of South Carolina. (These roses are named after Louis Noisette,

'Mme. Hardy' is a green-eyed enchantress in any American garden.

a Parisian who made further crosses and cultivars.)

The pioneers, Tom writes, left rose plants all across the Oregon Trail. Most likely they were 'Harison's Yellow', called the

THE PORTLAND ROSE FESTIVAL: DOING IT UP BIG

Portland, Oregon (the "Rose City") holds a week-long rose festival every year around the end of May. It began in 1888 and includes the "Portland's Best Rose" contest, a day-long parade of floats made of roses, food festivals, and big ships open for touring. They hold a huge rose competition with hundreds of awards that attracts gardeners and non-gardeners alike. A popular tradition brings the public flocking: At the end of the two-day show, the

judges and growers give away the roses to all comers. Rose Princesses represent each high school in the city and receive a college scholarship. A teen-aged Queen is selected to reign during the parade and the festivities.

The city also boasts one of the top seven municipal rose gardens in the world, including its International Rose Test Garden in Washington Park. (This garden has been nominated as the best rose garden in the world.)

A colonial garden in New Jersey.

"Yellow Rose of Texas" but first grown at the home of one Richard Harison, a New York attorney. If you want a complete rose history read, take up *In Search of Lost Roses*.

Grown in the USA
Everything's coming up roses.
Stephen Sondheim, 1959

America has a long history of rose growing. Many towns have municipal rose gardens. Cemeteries abound with roses. Festivals go on in cities and towns across the nation.

Growing roses in the United States means adapting them to a number of climates and conditions. We will discuss how these factors affect your choices in roses and the way you take care of them.

We'll also take a look at some of the growers and conditions across the nation. We

A lanky Climber in Carmel Mission, California.

'Harison's Yellow' growing near the mountains.

Wild roses endure in both city and country.

hope that you, as the reader and gardener, will be able to identify with rose growers of the past and of different regions, then apply their knowledge to yours. This leads us to the matter of climate.

Many gardeners live in climates with temperature ranges of 100 to 120 degrees Fahrenheit, and our plants have to deal with that to survive. When you think about it, it's remarkable to realize how many plants do survive despite nature's strict rules and tricks, not to mention all we do as gardeners to lay extra stress on our plants.

My colleagues in creating this book live all across the United States. We'll address the particular needs of gardeners in

Many Species roses are tough enough to handle our extreme U.S. climates.

Rosa banksiae lutea thrives in the heat of the South.

trying climates and pay special attention to how you can live with your particular growing conditions.

Where I come from we get everyone's weather. We get the South's warm, moist Gulf air (that helps mildew and black spot take hold); the Arctic

No mousy look in this garden! Standards of the Floribunda 'Showbiz'.

CUT ROSES: A BILLION-DOLLAR INDUSTRY

According to Jim Krone of Roses, Inc. (the trade association of the American cut rose industry), 1.2 billion cut roses are sold in the United States each year. That's 4 million sold every business day (six days/week). That equates to 333,333 bouquets of a dozen roses each day, or 41,666 dozens (half a million roses) sold every business hour.

With the average price of a cut rose estimated at $3.00, that's a daily figure of $12 million and an annual dollar figure of around $3.5 billion—for cut roses alone!

The Society of American Florists has 18,000 members in the U.S., primarily retail florists. Some 175 greenhouse growers supply the United States trade, which means that on the average each grower wholesales 7 million roses per year. By the way, 60 to 65 percent of cut roses are red—the "I Love You" color.

Circle blasts of winter (they can kill a tender plant in hours); big old Plains thunderstorms that can drop quarter-sized rainballs and occasional hail (a plant ravager of biblical fury). We also get long, warm, damp springs that can bring Pacific-Northwest style torrents. Spring often jumps right into the 100-degree days of July and August; often a drought comes in late summer too.

And that's just the predictable stuff!

Roses Are Big Business
What is fairer than a Rose?
What is sweeter?
George Herbert, 19th century

Rose growing is a significant component of the horticulture trade. Roses have a considerable economic impact and influence within the gardening world. In this book we'll draw on examples from the "business of roses" to show how the rose bush that we grow or the bouquet that we harvest is the product of a

TIP

According to the American Horticultural Society, things are changing, climate-wise:

• The average growing season in the 1990s was *seven to 11 days longer* than observed in the 1980s.

• *Five* of the 10 hottest years on record occurred in the 1990s.

• Steadily increasing levels of greenhouse gases—carbon dioxide—have been recorded with each passing year.

What's a gardener to do? We'll talk about working with your climate and local conditions so you can understand how best to work with nature.

The hips of Rosa rugosa *feed birds all across the continent.*

'Blaze' growing in Pennsylvania.

Roses in the right place improve any living space.

- More and more supermarkets and mass merchandisers carry flowers and have flower departments.
- Holidays and gifts account for 30 percent of all cut flower purchases, casual purchases 25 percent, hospital gifts 6 percent and bereavement purchases 15 percent.

The Right Rose in the Right Place

"I would never exchange one bloom of 'Mme. Hardy' for an armful of 'Iceberg'. Nor would I plant a bed of 'Mme. Hardy' in the middle of my lawn."

Peter Beales, Roses

Roses are excellent landscaping plants. In Chapter 4 we'll show you how to integrate roses into any landscape scheme and make for yourself a better living environment. Consider these facts:

worldwide horticultural network.

Today, record numbers of Americans are buying cut flowers, especially roses. Some background facts:

- Overall sales of cut flowers in the United States are near the $10 billion mark.
- More and more households purchase flowers at least once a month, more than ever before.

THE MORE THINGS CHANGE...

The boundless rose choices we have today are a measure of scale. In the United States, some 10,000 different rose cultivars and varieties are available to home gardeners. There are 80 million gardeners in the United States now. In 10 or 20 years we may have twice as many choices in roses, and twice as many gardeners.

To the Victorians, there was a seemingly unparalleled abundance of rose choices and uses. Typically, they took up their pens to describe them. In 1874 Dean S. Reynolds Hole wrote in his *A Book About Roses:*

"In a Rose-garden ... no formalism, no flatness, no monotonous repetition should prevail. There should the Rose be seen in all her multiform phases of beauty. There should be beds of Roses, banks of Roses, bowers of Roses, hedges of Roses, edgings of Roses, pillars of Roses, arches of Roses, fountains of Roses, baskets of Roses, vistas and alleys of the Rose. Now overhead and now at our feet, there they should creep and climb. New tints, new forms, new perfumes, should meet us at every turn."

If only those "stodgy Victorians" could show some enthusiasm once in a while!

Roses are strong partners with perennials in a mixed garden landscape.

Hundreds of rose varieties can be used in naturalized garden settings.

'Betty Prior' lends a carefree air to this relaxing garden.

'Flower Carpet Pink' is one of a new groundcover rose series.

From breeder to grower to nursery, roses are big business worldwide.

'Pink Meidiland' lends an old-timey feel to the garden with its single blossoms.

- A well-maintained landscape adds at least 15 percent to the value of a residential property.
- More than 88 percent of Americans feel that flowers and trees in a city are important beyond their pleasing appearance and their beauty.
- 40 percent of Americans say that being around plants makes them more calm and relaxed.
- Landscape design and good maintenance play a significant role in perceived and real security related to crime.

We'll give you an overview of the last 20 years of rose evolution, from the Hybrid Tea culture to today's wide-open marketplace of new, rediscovered and improved varieties and cultivars—a paradise for the home gardener. We'll emphasize such aspects of this evolution (or is it a revolution?) as the return of Old Roses, the David Austins, the rose rustling mentality (part of a new cultural history to rose growing), and the landscape class of non-fussy roses (such as Meidilands, and Flower Carpets).

Roses fit into almost any gardening philosophy or plan, and are enjoyable in a number of forms: as live blooms, cut flowers, landscape plants, display specimens, sources of fragrance, botanical forms, floral art, or even food and wildlife habitat resources in the form of rose hips and dense stalks. Roses offer a wide latitude of landscaping and artistic expression to the thoughtful gardener.

Roses really do offer a lot. They:

- Have a deservedly long and rich tradition.
- Are easy to grow when you follow certain basic principles.
- Offer many pleasurable features.
- Are a reliable plant in the right place.

'Charmian' is one of the David Austin English Roses that have transformed American gardens.

'Alba Semi-plena' is a sweetly scented rose that is more than 400 years old.

So, in the next chapter, let's take a brief journey through the way plant hybridizers and Mother Nature have constantly mixed different types of roses to create new kinds. This has led to a vast, almost bewildering variety of roses for us home gardeners to choose from today. We'll show you why rose growing has been so rewarding for centuries, and how it can be rewarding for you, the informed home gardener. Come on along!

Hybrid Teas are excellent flowers for cutting. This is 'Chrysler Imperial'.

'Scarlet Meidiland' is one of the disease-resistant new landscape roses.

The language of flowers begins with roses.

ROSELAWN: AN AMERICAN SAGA

The place I come from was dubbed "Roselawn" around 100 years ago. Just like some of our favorite roses, its story began overseas. A young German man, William Volker, left home in the 1880s to avoid conscription and seek his fortune. He moved to Chicago and started a business in home furnishings—window shades, picture frames and the like. He expanded in the Midwest, moved to Kansas City, Missouri, and made millions. But before he gave it all away to schools, hospitals and the indigent, he brought his family over to America...Mama, Papa, sisters and cousins.

The family needed more space, so William bought a 2-acre site with a four-bedroom house on the edge of town. They all moved in, and became famous around town: Mama for tending the family cow; Papa for growing wonderful roses on the grounds.

I wonder where Papa found the rose plants to grow. From a local gardener? Maybe he brought his own, or had cousin Johann send some from the Fatherland. At any rate, Papa Volker caught the "rose rage" as millions of new settlers and just plain gardeners have done.

Soon the place was christened "Roselawn" by the neighbors, and the Volkers proudly inscribed the tall stone pillars in the surrounding 3-foot-high wall. Then William caught the rose fever too, even marrying a small-town Kansas woman named Rose.

After a long, loving life, Rose and William passed away. The place changed hands and the famous roses lost ground to neglect. When I moved in on Thanksgiving Day, 1985, there were two wild rose bushes, and the place had no privacy. How could a place proclaim itself "Roselawn" and not have tons of roses to earn its lofty title? So I jumped headlong into growing roses.

I planted cuttings and shoots from the gardens where I worked. I accepted orphan plants from neighbors. I ordered from mail-order houses, especially those carrying old, landscape or shrub roses. I planted scores of them, including 'Celsiana', *Rosa* centifolia, 'Mme. Hardy', "Eglantine", 'Therese Bugnet', 'Climbing White Dawn', 'Othello' and 'Scarlet Meidiland', among others.

Now the place is rampant with roses among the trees and perennials. The main problem isn't bugs or black spot, it's curbing overzealous growth and choosing what to put in a vase next. The work's been repaid a thousand times by the beauty, fragrance, privacy and landscape value of the roses I've grown.

Just as they can in your garden, roses have once again made Roselawn a garden haven. And that's how I know that roses can transform *your* living space and make your efforts a part of a long, rich, American rose-growing tradition.

◈ CHAPTER 2 ◈

THE ROSE CHRONICLES: HOT HISTORY AND STEAMY SUBPLOTS

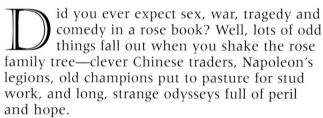

D id you ever expect sex, war, tragedy and comedy in a rose book? Well, lots of odd things fall out when you shake the rose family tree—clever Chinese traders, Napoleon's legions, old champions put to pasture for stud work, and long, strange odysseys full of peril and hope.

The "Yellow Rose of Texas" was planted by settlers but it sprang from a marriage between the Scotch Briars of Europe and *Rosa foetida* of western Asia. Don't tell this at the Lone Star Cafe, but this rose was discovered in a New York lawyer's garden.

The Climber we call the "Cherokee rose" was one of the first China roses brought back to Europe. Now it's the state flower of Georgia.

The roses we grow started in uncharted wilds. For centuries they've hybridized on their own or with a little help. In the late 1700s, British ships brought back "the four stud Chinas"—specimens that created a huge explosion in the rose world. Breeding of roses since 1792 has been based on the traits of repeat-blooming, yellow color and trailing or climbing habit. Just think: At one time, no Western-grown rose bloomed more than once a year. Now many gardeners spurn a rose that doesn't bloom all summer!

It's a tale that spans the ages.

THE CONQUERORS, EXPLORERS AND TRADERS

Roses have been a part of commerce as long as spices and silks. Plenty of evidence indicates that roses have been grown in China, Persia, western Asia and the Mediterranean for more than 5,000 years. We can make a good case that rose species were collected and spread as the great empires flourished and expanded.

Roses played a prominent role in both the Greek and Roman empires, whose builders and settlers certainly planted the genus throughout southern Europe, western Asia and Egypt. When the Arabs invaded Europe, they brought with them roses from ancient Persia. Roses were widely cultivated in medieval Europe, chiefly for their medicinal qualities but also for their usefulness in perfumes and for flavoring.

The Crusaders reportedly brought the first Damask Rose from Damascus to Europe in 1254, as well as perhaps the "Red Rose" (a Gallica) and Musk Roses.

Boatloads from China

The development of the merchant trade from the Far East to the Netherlands helped start today's worldwide commerce in horticulture and kicked off a huge turning point in rose history. For the first time, European growers saw and used specimens of the roses that the Chinese grew. One report says that the first China rose was received, perhaps as a dried specimen, by the Dutch botanist Gronovius in 1704. The introduction of roses and other flora from eastern Asia sparked the Dutch to take an interest in breeding, and they remained the West's preeminent breeders of roses

Empress Josephine's gardens at La Malmaison once were the Western world's most famous rose display.

The Bagatelle gardens are a Paris attraction.

until the French, sparked by the spoils of Napoleon's conquests, assumed supremacy in rose development in the 19th century.

The Europeans Take Over

While not an explorer herself, Napoleon's empress Josephine took advantage of the discoveries. Josephine had a profound effect upon the collection and subsequent development of roses from around the world. In 1804 she began collecting and growing every rose possible at her chateau at La Malmaison, near Paris. Napoleon's far-flung armies took care to collect and send to Malmaison roses from the countries they conquered. Josephine hired an English nurseryman, John Kennedy, who was allowed to travel between the warring countries for the purpose of consulting on the collection.

Reports say that shipments of Tea Roses from China to La Malmaison were protected by both sides during the height of the Napoleonic war between the French and the English.

The Church also took a hand in building Josephine's collections. French missionaries contributed, probably supplying the North American species recorded in the collections at La Malmaison.

The English were also clearly instrumental in opening up the rose world. The aggressive traders of the British East India Company played a large part during the 18th century in shipping roses from China and Persia to Europe, where their specimens were received with enthusiasm by breeders in the Netherlands and France as well as Great Britain. Many now-standard varieties and breeding stock came from these collective efforts.

Professional plant societies in Great Britain had an impact on the collection of roses from Asia.

TIP

A NOTE ON TERMINOLOGY:

All those odd punctuation marks help you understand just what you're reading.

- You know if a rose is a species because its name always begins *Rosa* (or *R.*), and the entire name is in **italics**: *Rosa rugosa*.
- Both varieties and cultivars are designated by **single quotes:** 'Pink Peace', 'Don Juan'. Varieties are technically a true-breeding form of a species in the wild, but the term is used more loosely in gardening circles to include any distinct form of a species or hybrid. "Cultivar" is a shortening of "cultivated variety" and means a plant that's the result of a man-made cross or a horticultural selection. We often use "variety" as the generic term for any man-made hybrid.
- **Double quotes** are used for unofficial common names or colloquial expressions: "Sweetbriar," "The Burglar Rose."

In the early 1800s, the Royal Horticultural Society at Kew sent William Kerr, a professional plant collector, to China. Kerr is credited with the discovery of the first double white rose, *R. banksiae alba plena*, called the "Lady Banks' Rose," which he found growing in gardens near Canton. This rose was shipped back to England in 1807 and has delighted rose growers with its scented, rosette-shaped flowers ever since.

In 1810 Sir Abraham Hume imported from the Fa Tee Nurseries in Canton a rose that's now officially called 'Hume's Blush Tea-scented China', the first of the Chinas to possess fragrance. E. H. Wilson ("Chinese Wilson," the legendary plant explorer) is credited with discovering many China Roses in the 1890s and early 1900s. Wilson introduced *R. moyesii*, known for its large vase-shaped hips, in 1908.

In 1817 the French botanist Breon, director of a modest botanical garden on the Isle de Bourbon (now called Reunion) in the Indian Ocean, collected seeds of a rose used as a hedge on the island and sent them to friends in France. From this came the first Bourbon rose. This rose is thought to be a cross between a prolific pink China Rose (probably 'Old Blush') and *R. damascena bifera* (the 'Autumn Damask'). The fertile seeds Breon collected led to the development of a large group of tried-and-true garden varieties including 'Souvenir de la Malmaison', 'Boule de Neige', and one of my favorites, the headily fragrant 'Mme. Isaac Pereire'.

The Royal Horticultural Society sent John Parks to Asia in search of roses and other flora in 1823. He brought back 'Parks' Yellow Tea-scented China' as well as the "Yellow Banksia" rose, *R. banksiae lutea*. The species *R. banksiae* was named after him.

Shaking the Rose Family Tree

Before we take a brief stroll through rose lineage, it helps to remember that roses are classified in three general groups:

1) **Species Roses**—All other roses descend from Species roses. These are roses that breed true (offspring exactly like parent) when bred with themselves or others from the same species. They were originally found growing in the wild. You can still grow them in lots of garden settings. Many of our Shrub Roses are closely related to Species.

2) **Old Roses**—Also known as Old Garden Roses (OGR). These are groups and classes of roses whose varieties and cultivars were grown before the development of the first Hybrid Tea rose in 1867. (Don't be confused to hear of a new Old Rose. We're still breeding them from the stock of the pre-1867 OGRs and their descendants.)

3) **Modern Roses**—These are roses developed since 1867, when French nurseryman Jean-Baptiste Guillot introduced the first Hybrid Tea, 'La France'.

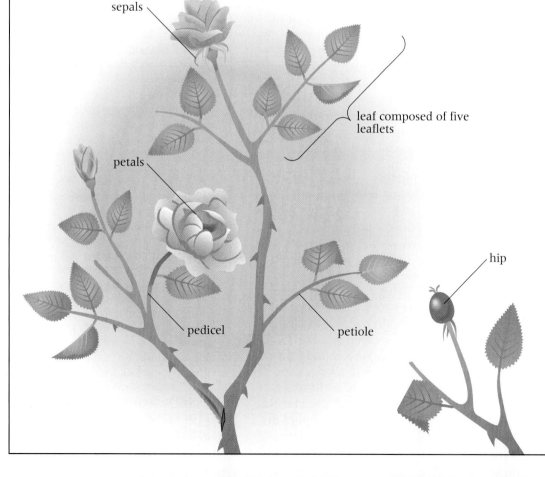

sepals

leaf composed of five leaflets

petals

pedicel

petiole

hip

The main parts of a rose plant have evolved through the centuries.

SPECIES ROSES

The "Cherokee Rose," Rosa laevigata, *is a Species rose native to China.*

Species roses are the ancestors of the genus, providing the foundation for all roses. Botanists list from 150 to 200 species of roses. This is a wide-ranging number owing partly to the difficulty in figuring out the exact characteristics defining a species, but also to the lack of definitive historical evidence for telling a true species and a simple variation within a species. There's always some reclassification going on.

What we do know is that these ancestral species are characterized by single, five-petaled blossoms (except for one four-petaled one, *R. sericea)*. They're usually fragrant, which makes sense since they've had to attract natural pollinators in the wild. Most of them have thorns or "prickles" that protect them from predators. They've all originated in the northern hemisphere.

Species roses range in size from diminutive shrubs to sweeping climbers, with a color range from white to shades of pink to dark red, as well as yellow; the size and shape of their leaves, thorns and hips are likewise varied.

It's easier to understand Species roses if we group them by their geographical origin:

China/Asia

For over 200 years, Asiatic Species have been central to creating the roses we know today. Important characteristics of Asiatic species are: their genetic trait for reblooming, known as "remontancy"; their use as the source of yellow-colored flowers; and the habits of trailing or climbing.

Let's look at four Asiatic species that have been especially important in the breeding of Old and Modern Roses, and see how they relate to what we grow today:

1. *R. chinensis* (China), the "China Rose." This rose is recognized as the great-great-granddaddy of all modern species. It has a climbing habit; its single flowers of rich pink maturing to dark crimson bloom once per season. Sadly, this species is now believed to be extinct in the wild.

2. *R. gigantea* (China), the "Giant Rose." This is the rose that first carried the "tea" scent. In its wild form it grows to a height of 40 feet or more, with lemon-white flowers that are 5 inches across.

3. *R. wichuraiana* (Japan, Korea, China). A short climber or dense shrub with shiny, dark, almost evergreen foliage. It makes a great groundcover and is an important parent of many widely used hybrid climbing roses including 'American Pillar', 'Blaze', 'Dorothy Perkins' and 'New Dawn'.

4. *R. multiflora*, also known as *R. polyantha* (Japan, Korea). This is a principal parent of several major classes of roses—

Floribunda, Hybrid Musks, Polyanthas, Modern Shrubs and Modern Climbers among them. Known also as a rootstock for nursery budding. A dense climber with lots of single, creamy white flowers followed by small red hips, it's a good candidate for an informal hedgerow.

Other interesting Asiatic species that enrich our gardening choices include the following:

R. banksiae (Asia), "Lady Banks' Rose." A vigorous rose with a climbing habit and white to yellow flowers. Among the oldest living rose plants is an enormous Lady Banks' rose in Tombstone, Arizona. Hardy to Zone 8.

R. rugosa (Japan, China, Korea). An extremely hardy, bushy rose that thrives in sandy soil. The species includes a variety of colors and large rose hips. Some have fragrance. Rugosas are very hardy and disease-resistant. Minor drawbacks include prickly stems (which do make them good hedges) and the fact that the flowers do not last long, although some rebloom.

R. moyesii (Western China). Known for its intense red flowers, magnificent flagon-shaped hips and a tall habit. This is a very popular Species rose, even today.

R. laevigata (China). The "Cherokee rose" is a climber with nearly evergreen foliage and creamy-white flowers. Zone 7.

R. roxburghii (China and Japan), the "Burr" or "Chestnut" rose. This is a rigid and prickly plant. Bees love its shell-pink flowers. It's also known for its hips, which are covered in prickles. Zone 6.

R. hugonis (Central China), the "Golden Rose of China" or "Father Hugo's Rose." Nearly thornless, its tiny, smooth leaves create a fernlike effect and the butter-yellow flowers bloom in early spring. This large bush grows to 10 feet in rocky, semi-arid climates. Zone 6.

R. bracteata (China), the "Macartney Rose." This climbing rose is not very hardy, but oddly enough will often do well on a north wall. It does well in the southern United States, sometimes too well: planting it is prohibited in Texas, where it naturalizes too easily. 'Mermaid' is a popular cultivar.

Europe/Mediterranean

From the balmier regions of Europe and the Mediterranean basin come four species that are important ancestors of Old Roses and Modern Roses:

1. *R. moschata* (Mediterranean), the "Musk Rose." A Climber, its flowers turn from cream to white at the end of the summer and into autumn, carrying a sweet scent.

2. *R. canina* (Britain, Europe). A wild rose found throughout Europe, the "Dog Rose" has wonderful pale pink flowers with a sweet fragrance. Its hips are particularly high in vitamin C and are even used for wine! *R. canina* is also known for its part in the development of the Alba (white) roses, and its use as a rootstock. Zone 4.

3. *R. phoenicea* (Turkey, Syria). Principally known as one of the parents of the "Damask Rose" and, generations later, the "Cabbage Rose."

4. *R. gallica* (Mediterranean). The "Red Rose," sometimes known as *R. rubra*. Although *R. gallica* is also classified as an Old Rose, the ancestral Red Rose is a foundation species that has been around for centuries. It was first mentioned by Pliny in 79 A.D. Its inclination to mutate naturally and its ease of hybridization make its origin difficult to trace. *R. gallica officinalis*, one of its hybrids, is one of the most storied roses ever. Known as 'Apothecary's Rose' and the "Red Rose of Lancaster," the long-lasting scent of its petals has been used for ages in herbal medicine, perfumes and cosmetics. 'Rosa Mundi' is a famous striped variety.

North America

While the 30 or so North American species have not played a major role in the development of Old and Modern Roses, there are two notable natives:

R. setigera, the "Prairie Rose," a Climber discovered in 1810. When crossed with *R. gallica* and others, it has been a parent of some

Many roses that naturalize in the wild provide breeding stock for today's roses.

notable hybrid climbers introduced by American breeders, such as 'Queen of the Prairies' and 'Baltimore Belle' (both introduced in 1843), and several Horvath hybrids, including 'Captain Kidd', 'Doubloons', 'Jean Lafitte' (all 1934) and 'American Pillar' (1902). Zone 3.

R. virginiana, a member of the family *Carolinae* found throughout the wilds in the United States and Canada. Probably the most notable offspring of this group is *R. virginiana plena*, also known as 'Rose d'Amour' or "St. Mark's Rose," exceptional in its deepening pink flowers and late-blooming habit. Zone 4.

Other Noteworthy Species

R. glauca (mountains of central and southern Europe), formerly known as *R. rubrifolia*.

Best known for the soft mauve/violet coloring of its shoots and leaves. Open growing, to 6 to 8 feet, with purple-red hips borne in clusters. It shows its best foliage color in partial shade. Zone 2.

R. pimpinellifolia (Europe), the "Scotch Rose" or "Scotch Briar." Formerly known as *R. spinosissima*. The German house of Kordes created several wonderful trouble-free, upright hybrids that often are our first bloomers. These include 'Frühlingsgold' ("Spring Gold") and 'Frühlingsmorgen' ("Spring Morning"). Another familiar hybrid of this species is the brightly hued 'Harison's

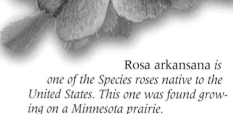

Rosa arkansana is one of the Species roses native to the United States. This one was found growing on a Minnesota prairie.

Yellow' (ca. 1830), the "Yellow Rose of Texas."

R. foetida (Western Asia), the "Austrian Briar." The source of the yellow color in Hybrid Teas, Hybrid Perpetuals and other Modern Roses. Also known as *R. lutea. R. foetida bicolor*, "Austrian Copper," is a sport that has intense copper-orange flowers. As you might tell from its name, the species has a somewhat unpleasant fragrance, but by and large that's been bred out of its garden offspring.

R. eglanteria (Europe), the "Sweetbriar" or "Eglantine." A multi-branched, sometimes unruly shrub, it makes up for its growth habit with the sweet fragrance of its foliage and clear pink flowers. Useful as an impenetrable hedge.

R. sempervirens (southern Europe/northern Africa). A nearly evergreen climber that has bred such useful offspring as 'Félicité et Perpétue' and 'Spectabile'.

Roses being tested at the U.S. National Arboretum.

BREEDING BREAKTHROUGHS FOR THE HOME GARDENER

The vast rose propagating fields at Jackson & Perkins, birthplace of many famous roses.

Over the centuries, various kinds of roses have come in and out of fashion. Whole classes of roses (Hybrid Teas, Shrubs) and certain individual varieties ('Peace', 'Dortmund') have become very popular. Like Academy Award and Grammy winners, roses get the gardening spotlight when new breakthroughs win major awards. For instance, when 'Bonica' became the first shrub rose to win the coveted All American Rose Selections (AARS) award, sales soared.

But soon the "new and improved" varieties such as 'Royal Bonica' replaced it in many catalogs.

So some roses stay popular; some fade into obscurity. 'Peace' was introduced to the U.S. market by Conard Pyle in 1946, and is now more popular than ever. But during that same time, thousands of roses have debuted, only to have their popularity (and sales) fade like a spent blossom. Some of it depends on simple things like a rose's name. Most

'Peace' was a breakthrough in breeding, and one of the most popular roses ever.

'Simplicity' shows the Floribunda trait of clusters of flowers. They also have the repeat-blooming habit.

developing new Hybrid Teas—producing unique flower colorings, bud quality and long-stemmed growth habits. But times have changed. Many gardeners have become discouraged by Hybrid Teas' notorious need for high-maintenance, high-expense spraying and pruning, not to mention their unattractiveness as a plant, blooms aside. More recent work has produced a resurgence of interest in Old Roses, and the development of new roses that blend modern traits with the beautiful flower forms and fragrance of Old Roses.

We rose gardeners are reaping the rewards of efforts begun in the middle of the 20th century. The pace really took off in Europe in the 1960s and expanded to North America in the next decade, when rose hybridizers started concentrating on producing roses with better disease resistance, new growth habits, novel flower coloration and improved fragrance. Three prime examples that showcase this trend come to mind: David Austin's work with English Roses, now almost a household word among gardeners; the French house of Meilland's versatile "Meidiland" landscape shrubs; and the disease-resistant groundcover roses like the "Flower Carpet" series.

The New Pioneers

Two award-winning American rose breeders typify these new directions. Tom Carruth, hybridizer at Weeks Roses in California, notes that today's breeders are working to develop roses with flower

of it depends on the way people are gardening, which helps drive the market and reinforces the value of the hybridizer's work.

Roses continue to grow in popularity, which is a measure of the widening recognition of the many great qualities they offer to the home gardener. Much of their popularity is due to the good instincts and hard work of our modern hybridizers. They're the ones who are working to breed those great qualities into our new roses.

The Limelight Shifts to New Stars

Up until the last 25 years or so, hybridizers had focused on

Ralph Moore, one of the foremost American Miniature breeders, in his test greenhouse.

Keith Zary is an award-winning breeder at Jackson & Perkins.

'Climbing Fourth of July' by Weeks Roses was the first Climber to win an AARS award in 23 years.

forms different from the classic Hybrid Tea—for example, single, fully double, and cupped forms. Keith Zary, hybridizer at Jackson & Perkins, says that the biggest change in modern rose development is breeding Modern Roses with an old-fashioned look and fragrance.

Breeders also are developing roses that are more versatile landscape plants and which offer season-long interest. Zary notes that Jackson & Perkins is emphasizing development of Shrub-type roses, such as J & P's "Simplicity" series. These roses provide home gardeners additional opportunities to use roses outside of formal rose beds. At Jackson & Perkins, 50 percent of the business is devoted to roses for the home gardener. The other major portion of its effort is devoted to plants for the cut-flower trade.

Many of the new roses are being grown on their own roots, rather than grafted onto other rootstock. Own-root roses enjoy better vigor and cold hardiness.

Work under way to improve disease resistance is also helping make roses a more popular plant choice for home gardens. Modern rose breeders have been influenced by the "green movement" and are working to reduce or eliminate the need for the chemical sprays traditionally used to control disease.

Jack Christensen of Armstrong Nursery in California.

'Graham Thomas' is part of the rose revolution of the late 20th century.

The test fields at Heirloom Old Garden Roses in St. Paul, Oregon.

Roses Down the Road

What's next in rose development? Certainly we can expect to see a continuation of the ongoing work to blend the best qualities of the old with the new. Landscape roses will continue to be popular with the home gardener. Miniatures will always be in style because they fit just about any gardening style or situation.

Responding to the needs and preferences of home gardeners will keep the breeders and hybridizers busy working on roses with improved vigor and disease resistance.

Extending blooming time and adding fragrance to roses that lack only a nice scent will also be possibilities, as they have been for ages.

Can we breed a rose that will withstand both Arctic blasts and an Alabama summer? Maybe! Some experts say that the next big revolution in rose development is likely to be the use of genetic engineering in breeding. That may or may not improve our chances of ever finding roses that laugh at black spot or Japanese beetles. But it may open up the door to more off-the-wall experimentation: Are we ready for roses with flowers the size of basketballs?

MINIS ARE MOVING UP, UP, UP

John Saville, of Nor'East Miniature Roses, based in Massachusetts, notes that interest in Miniature roses has "taken off" and continues to grow. He credits this new interest in Minis to the abundance of flower colors and plant forms developed in recent decades. Both Saville and Jerry Justice, of Oregon's Justice Miniature Roses, add that the gardening community sees that Miniatures offer a lot. They add versatility in the placement of roses in the garden, they outbloom their larger relatives, they're tough, and they're relatively easy to grow. All this makes them perfect for new home gardeners to reap early successes with roses.

Saville is the son of legendary Miniature rose breeder Harm Saville, who began the business as a hobby almost 30 years ago. Today Nor'East sells over 500,000 Miniatures a year. John Saville says that his nursery is working to develop Miniatures with more fragrance and frequent blooms. 'Scentsation' is a breakthrough in fragrance found in a Miniature rose, he says, while 'Rainbow's End', a beautiful yellow and red bicolor, is the nursery's most popular Mini.

By the way, we'd have no Miniatures at all but for *R. chinensis minima*, which carried the dominant trait for dwarfing.

◄ CHAPTER 3 ►
VARIETIES: SO MANY CHOICES

Thousands and thousands of rose varieties, each one tempting you with its exquisite catalog description or inviting nursery tag. How do you, the home gardener, choose just a tiny fraction, just the ones that will work best? The secret is in knowing what each rose variety has to offer.

In this chapter we break down that seemingly endless list of varieties into a more manageable number of categories. You'll then find it much easier to select the best ones for your own particular interests.

Take a little time to study the growing and blooming habits, as well as the pluses and minuses of each rose classification. This will help you focus on those rose varieties that best suit your climate, different landscaping needs, maintenance requirements and personal preferences for color, fragrance and style.

ROSE CATEGORIES:
A MAP OF EACH FAMILY'S HABITS

Hybrid Tea 'Fragrant Cloud'.

The classic red Hybrid Tea 'Mister Lincoln'.

The categories on the following pages—official classifications of roses as designated by the American Rose Society—each represent a group of roses with similar characteristics and, perhaps, a common lineage. For example, a Floribunda rose is the result of a cross between a Hybrid Tea and a Polyantha. So if you see that a rose is a Floribunda, you can expect it to be bushy, with flowers produced in sprays throughout the growing season. (Because roses can be cross-pollinated so readily, not only are new varieties continually being developed but also new categories. Any distinctive new plant form, flower form or other characteristic can be the basis of a new class of roses.)

Species Roses (pp. 21–23) offer many gardening choices. The other two broad categories are Old Garden Roses and Modern Roses. Old Garden Roses are those types that existed before 1867, the year that the first Hybrid Tea was introduced.

Even if a new variety is created today, if its characteristics are that of one of the classes of Old Garden Roses, then that is its classification.

With the introduction of the Hybrid Tea 'La France' in 1867, Modern Roses were born. Throughout much of the 20th

Fragrant Hybrid Rugosa 'Blanc Double de Coubert'.

'Dainty Bess', a versatile Hybrid Tea.

century, gardeners were most drawn by the Hybrid Tea roses with their almost constant production of long-stemmed, high-centered blooms. But there are a number of other classes as well. The attributes most notable among the Modern Roses include a tendency to have a wide range of bright colors and continual bloom.

'Double Delight', a highly rated Hybrid Tea.

'Nastarana', a fragrant Noisette.

'Blaze', a Large-Flowered Climber, adorns a traditional white picket fence.

A DIP INTO THE GENE POOL

The roses we are familiar with today are the product—and the breeding stock—of centuries of natural and man-made genetic development.

1) Rosa foetida, *the"Austrian briar," came from the Middle East no later than the 16th century.* R. foetida *and* R. foetida bicolor *have sired vigorous Climbers and Shrubs. The two are also responsible for yellow tones in today's roses.*

2) Rosa foetida bicolor, *or "Austrian Copper," sported from* R. foetida *and brought orange into the rose palette.*

3) *'Félicité Parmentier', a wonderful Alba, was created sometime around 1830. Albas go back at least to medieval days and are probably descended from the Dog Rose,* R. canina, *and either* R. gallica *or one of the Damasks.*

4) *'Hermosa' is an excellent China rose that was developed in France around 1840. Through the China lineage we enjoy several important traits in our roses, including repeat bloom, climbing, yellow flower tones (through combinations with* R. foetida*) and miniaturization.*

OLD ROSES

Old Roses include those classifications of roses that were in existence prior to 1867, the year that 'La France' (the first Hybrid Tea rose) was introduced. They come from all parts of the world and offer a diversity of flower and plant shapes, fragrance, pest resistance and hardiness. Many of them make outstanding Shrubs for the landscape.

Learning the characteristics of each class of Old Roses will help you choose the best ones for your gardening needs. Here's a brief survey of Old Roses.

Alba

The Romans grew the Albas 2,000 years ago and brought them to Britain where, by the Middle Ages, they were used for medicinal purposes. The refinement and beauty of the shrubs fit in well with today's gardens. The leaves are blue-green or gray-green on vigorous, upright growth that is pest-resistant and long-lived, even surviving light shade and difficult conditions. Plants grow 4 to 8 feet tall, and have few thorns and large hips. The 3-inch, semidouble or double, white or pink, uniquely fragrant flowers appear once in midsummer. Albas do best on their own roots, spreading slowly by runners, sometimes surviving even to Zone 3. Most flowers are produced on two-year-old wood.

"*Yellow Lady Banks' Rose,*" R. banksiae lutea, *creates a stunning display.*

Climbing 'New Dawn' is a reliable performer on a trellis or arch.

'Maiden's Blush', a wonderful Alba.

'Altissimo', a single-flowered repeat-blooming Climber.

'Zéphirine Drouhin', a stunning Bourbon rose, growing with delphiniums.

Bourbon

The original Bourbon was found in 1817 on the Ile de Bourbon, now Reunion Island, in the Indian Ocean. It was a natural cross between the China ('Old Blush') and *Rosa damascena* var. *bifera* ('Autumn Damask'). Bourbon Roses were very popular in the 1800s, with many cultivars developed by further crosses with Gallicas and Damasks.

Plants range in size from less than 6 feet to over 15 feet tall. Richly fragrant, the 3- to 4-inch flowers are very double, with quartered centers, in colors of white, pink, maroon, purple, crimson or striped. Most varieties rebloom, especially if pruned back one-third after the first flowering. Plants have thick, strong canes with large, glossy, bright green leaves that are sometimes susceptible to mildew and black spot. Bourbons do best in full sun with rich, moist soil and are hardy to Zone 6.

'Old Blush', a China rose with many offspring, including the Bourbon Roses.

'Summer Damask', a descendant of the roses brought back to Europe by the Crusaders.

Centifolias are prized for their very double, quartered, button-centered flowers of pink, white, crimson, purple or mauve. Blooming once during midsummer, the flowers have a rich, intense, heady fragrance. Depending on the cultivar, Centifolias grow 3 to 6 feet tall with thin, thorny stems forming open bushes. The taller-growing types often need staking. The large, rounded, wrinkly, gray-green leaves are susceptible to black spot and mildew. Plants take several years to become established and need full sun and rich, moist soil. Hardy to Zone 4, they should be pruned back lightly after flowering.

regular feeding, watering and light pruning, they will bloom almost continuously.

Centifolia

Often referred to as the Cabbage or Provence rose, Centifolias are natural hybrids from southern Europe. Originating before the 1600s,

'Autumn Damask', also known as "Quatre Saisons" ("Four Seasons"), has been used for potpourri for centuries. It was the first rose in Europe to produce flowers twice in a season.

China

Native to China and brought to Europe and England in the late 1700s, China roses are crucial to the rose world because they contributed the repeat-blooming trait, plus yellow color, to breeding efforts. Stems are delicate and twiggy, with few thorns and sparse, shiny, light semi-green leaves. Growing 3 to 6 feet tall, China roses are disease-resistant, tolerant of alkaline soil, long-lived but hardy only to Zone 7. The single or loosely double flowers, in shades of red, apricot, yellow, pink and white, are not affected by high humidity. With

'Jeanne de Montfort', a Moss Rose.

R. macrantha, *a fragrant Species Rose.*

The "Prairie Rose," R. setigera, *is one of the few North American natives. It's hardy to Zone 3.*

'Baronne Prévost', a Hybrid Perpetual.

Damask

Since ancient Persia, Damask roses have enticed with their haunting fragrance. The petals are used to make attar of roses for perfume. Most Damasks are once-blooming except for the 'Autumn Damask' (R. *damascena* var. *bifera*) and varieties bred from it. The nodding sprays of semidouble or double pink or white flowers are centered with golden stamens. Plants range in size from 3 to 7 feet, with thorny, arching stems. The gray-green leaves are deeply veined and downy on the underside. Damasks are hardy through Zone 4 and do best in rich, moist soil and full sun.

Gallica

Gallicas were the first roses to be cultivated in Western civilizations, grown in the 12th century B.C. by the Medes and Persians. The ancient Romans used the blooms medicinally and spread the plants throughout their empire. As the principal parent of many of the Old Garden Roses, Gallicas dominated Empress Josephine's collection.

Gallica roses are hardy through Zone 4, with upright to arching slender, bristly stems growing 3 to 5 feet tall that spread by suckers when grown on their own roots. The species has single, fragrant, bright pink flowers, while the cultivars may be single or double and mauve, pink, red-purple, maroon or blush, sometimes marbled or mottled. Flowers are produced for about six weeks in early summer. Single and semidouble cultivars produce hips in the fall. The rough, dark green

'White Dawn', a Large-Flowered Climber.

foliage is somewhat susceptible to mildew in hot, dry weather.

Although tolerant of poor soils, Gallicas do best with good growing conditions. They are good plants for the shrub border or interplanted with old-fashioned flowers, but the canes may need support, especially during flowering. The fragrant petals are good to use in potpourri.

SOME HIGHLY RATED DAMASKS

'Celsiana', 4' x 3'; semidouble, light pink, fragrant flowers with golden stamens; blooms for long period; showy hips.

'Mme. Hardy', 5' x 5'; double, white, fragrant flowers with green button eye.

'Mme. Zöetmans', 4' x 3'; double, soft pink, fragrant flowers with green button eye.

'Marie Louise', 4' x 3'; double deep pink fragrant flowers with green button eye.

Repeat-blooming varieties include:

'Autumn Damask', 4' x 4'; double, pink, fragrant flowers; sprawling canes need support.

'Rose de Rescht', 3' x 3'; double, deep crimson-pink, fragrant flowers with button eye; vigorous but neat.

'Communis', a variety of R. centifolia muscosa; *like all Mosses, it is highly scented.*

SOME HIGHLY RATED GALLICAS

'Apothecary's Rose', 3' x 3'; double, magenta-crimson, fragrant flowers with yellow stamens; showy hips; 'Rosa Mundi' is a sport with palely striped flowers and 'Camaieux' is a cultivar with darker stripes.

'Complicata', 5' x 3'; single, deep pink, fragrant flowers with a white eye and yellow stamens; dense foliage and showy orange hips; can be used as a climber; slightly less hardy than other Gallicas.

'Empress Josephine', 3' x 3'; semidouble, fragrant, deep pink flowers flushed with purple and with dark veins; gray-green leaves; turban-shaped hips.

'James Mason', 5' x 4'; semidouble, fragrant, deep red flowers with gold stamens; hybrid developed in the 20th century; urn-shaped hips; can be used as a climber.

'Superb Tuscan', 4' x 3'; double, fragrant, dark crimson-maroon flowers with golden stamens; also listed as 'Tuscany Superb'.

'Frühlingsanfang', one of the tough Hybrid Spinosissimas.

Hybrid Perpetual

The Hybrid Perpetuals were produced from crosses of the Autumn Damasks, Bourbons, and Chinas in the mid- to late 1800s. Varieties range from short bushes to tall shrubs that can be trained as climbers.

Mostly double and fragrant, the flowers may be shades of pink, maroon or white, blooming in early summer, then again in the fall. They do best with rich, moist but well-drained soil and regular pruning, as new growth produces the most flowers. Hybrid Perpetuals are hardy through Zone 4.

The Hybrid Foetida 'Harison's Yellow' is one of the season's first bloomers.

Hybrid Spinosissima

Better known as Scotch or Burnet roses, these hybrids are derived from *R. spinosissima* (formerly known as *R. pimpinellifolia*). The species was originally found in Scotland, but it also grows in Europe and Asia. Both the species and hybrids are known for their toughness, cold-hardiness, adaptability and disease resistance. The arching, slender stems are covered with small bristles and delicate, fernlike leaves. Scotch roses will spread if grown on their own roots or if the graft union is buried. The single, semidouble or double flowers have a unique scent and may be once- or repeat-blooming in shades of white, pink and yellow. Hardiness varies from Zone 3 to 5.

SOME HIGHLY RATED HYBRID PERPETUALS

'Baronne Prévost', 5' x 4'; double, fragrant, rose-pink flowers; blooms over a long period.

'Ferdinand Pichard', 5' x 4'; double, fragrant flowers with red and pink stripes; few thorns.

'Frau Karl Druschki', 6' x 4'; double, high-centered, white flowers; can be used as a climber.

'Mrs. John Laing', 4' x 3'; double, fragrant, pink flowers.

'Reine des Violettes', 5' x 3'; very double, fragrant, rare mauve-violet flowers; nearly thornless.

SOME HIGHLY RATED HYBRID SPINOSISSIMAS

'Frühlingsmorgen', 6' x 5'; single, fragrant, repeat-blooming, creamy white flowers blushed with red and centered with golden-brown stamens; large red hips; Zone 5.

'Karl Forster', 5' x 4'; semidouble, repeat-blooming, white flowers; Zone 5. A classic variety.

'Stanwell Perpetual', 5' x 5'; double, fragrant, repeat-blooming, pale pink flowers; Zone 3.

'Reine des Violettes', a fragrant Hybrid Perpetual hardy to Zone 4.

'Duchesse de Brabant', a fragrant Tea Rose.

SOME HIGHLY RATED MOSSES

'Communis', 4' x 3'; very double, quartered, button-centered, once-blooming, fragrant, pink flowers; thick, red moss on buds and stems; disease-resistant; thorny.

'Crested Moss', 5' x 4'; very double, fragrant, once-blooming, pink flowers; green moss only on bud tips; thorny; may need support.

'Henri Martin', 5' x 4'; double, fragrant, once-blooming, crimson flowers fade to deep rose; bright green moss.

'Salet', 4' x 3'; double, fragrant, repeat-blooming, rose-pink flowers; red moss on buds; bristly, arching canes.

'William Lobb', 8' x 5'; double, fragrant, once-blooming, dark crimson-purple flowers with white centers; thick moss; bristly, thorny canes need support; can be used as a climber.

'Crested Moss' is also known as "Châpeau de Napoléon" because to some it looks like a cocked hat.

Moss

Moss Roses derive their name from the textured, resin-scented growth on the outside of the flower buds. These roses are natural sports, mainly from Centifolias but also a few from 'Autumn Damask'. Although the sports were found in the 1600s, their height of popularity was not until the mid-1800s. Some bloom only once a year, but those that have been crossed with Chinas have repeat bloom. The 1- to 3-inch flowers are usually fully double, fragrant, in shades of pink, red or white, and borne in clusters.

Most Moss Roses are hardy through Zone 4. They do best in rich, moist but well-drained soil.

Rosa centifolia, the "Cabbage Rose," lends a timeless air to any garden.

'La Reine Victoria', a silky-petaled Bourbon.

'Golden Showers', a fragrant Climber in a mixed border.

Noisette

Created in the early 1800s in South Carolina by John Champney, the Noisettes were the first class of roses originating in the United States. They are the result of a cross between the Musk Rose (*R. moschata*) and the China rose (*R. chinensis*). Further crosses were made with Bourbon, China and Tea Roses by Louis Noisette in Paris.

As tall, graceful, repeat-blooming Shrubs and Climbers, Noisettes are among the best of the Old Roses for the South and other warmer climates through Zone 7. The fragrant, double flowers, borne in clusters, are in shades of pink, cream or yellow. Plants are somewhat susceptible to black spot and mildew.

Tea

By crossing China roses with Bourbons and Noisettes, the Tea roses were developed in the 19th century. Tea Roses are generally

'The Fairy', a Polyantha, will often bloom all season and is a good performer as a groundcover or in a massed planting.

'Great Maiden's Blush' is a classic Alba that carries a fine perfume.

"Austrian Copper," R. foetida bicolor, *is a Species rose that brings orange into the rose palette.*

SOME HIGHLY RATED NOISETTES

'Blush Noisette', 8' x 6'; double, fragrant, pale pink flowers; nearly thornless; use as a climber or shrub.

'Jaune Desprez', 18' x 12'; double, quartered, fragrant, yellow flowers shaded apricot and a green eye; use as a climber.

'Rêve d'Or', 12' x 8'; double, fragrant, yellow flowered tinged with peach; use as a climber.

'Rosa Mundi' (R. gallica versicolor), *the striped Gallica rose, is a sport of the fabled R.* gallica officinalis, *the "Apothecary Rose."*

SWEETBRIAR: WORTH EVERY SCENT

One of my rose gardening mentors, Fred Leimkuhler, grew a tough-looking specimen that had big old thorns on strong, sturdy canes. While it had nice blooms, they were gone in a few weeks. One day Fred, sensing that I was feeling ho-hum about this plant, said "Come here. I'll show you something really unusual." He took a fingerful of leaves from this rose bush and rubbed them together. "Smell this," he said.

A waft of green apple scent hit me as I leaned toward the leaves. Fred had introduced me to the "Sweetbrier" or "Eglantine," a very special rose for many reasons.

Rosa eglanteria is the ancestor for all Eglantines. They've come from Europe and have been around for centuries. Shakespeare wrote of the Eglantine. It's not the showiest of roses, but it offers several redeeming qualities:

- Scented leaves: During a rainfall, the apple scent floats all around the Eglantine. The first rose I planted at Roselawn was *Rosa eglanteria*, to screen the porch from the view of passersby. To this day—many years later—there's nothing that compares to sitting on the front porch swing in the summer during a welcome rainstorm. The scent of apples fills the air and makes everything cooler and sweeter. 'Cox's Orange Pippin' is the apple variety that carries this scent, Fred says.
- Nice flowers: The single, light pink flowers often have a yellow eye. Bees love them.
- Handy uses: As I found, Eglantine is a great screen plant. It's even better as a hedge plant. Aggressive thorns and thick canes will keep out anything short of armor-clad knights. It grows 6-12 feet tall and just as wide. Plant a row of them downwind from your summertime sitting spot, and let the wind carry the scent of the leaves.
- Heavy hips: Sweetbriar develops large, nickel- to quarter-size orange hips. For the sake of the birds, I hope that most bushes don't have porcupine-like prickly hips like mine does.

slender, twiggy, upright plants with few thorns. The flowers may be single, semidouble, or double, with most rose colors except for deep yellow and dark red. The name of this class is derived from the fragrance.

Tea roses bloom for a long period in early summer, then again later in the season. They are hardy through Zone 7 and survive the heat of the South and West Coasts well.

"Yellow Lady Banks' Rose" blooms in clusters.

A multipetaled "Cabbage Rose," R. centifolia.

SOME HIGHLY RATED TEAS

'Duchesse de Brabant', 4' x 3'; double, fragrant, pink flowers; hardier than other Tea Roses.

'Maman Cochet', 3' x 2'; double, fragrant, high-centered pink flower; nearly thornless; climbing, white, and red forms available.

'Perle des Jardins', 4' x 3'; double, fragrant, yellow flower; climbing form available.

'Sombreuil', 10' x 6'; double, fragrant, creamy white flowers; large thorns; use as a climber.

MODERN ROSES

Legend has it that the first and only specimens of the incomparable Hybrid Tea 'Peace' were flown out on the last plane to leave France before the Germans invaded.

For much of the 20th century, gardeners focused most of their interest in roses on the Modern Roses, especially the Hybrid Teas, Grandifloras, and Floribundas. These types of roses offer high-centered blooms with thick petals in a wide range of colors, blends and bicolors. Perhaps most important, Modern Roses produce flowers almost all season long.

In recent years, there has been a backlash against these types because of their susceptibility to diseases, lack of hardiness and stiff appearance in the landscape. Still, the home gardener should try to accommodate the best of the Modern Roses, because of their unique beauty.

Hybrid Tea

For many people, "Hybrid Tea" and "Rose" are equivalent. To have a single narrow, high-centered bud on a sturdy stem has become the height of modern rose beauty. The first Hybrid Tea rose, 'La France', was the result of a cross between a Hybrid Perpetual and a Tea Rose. It offered compact growth and reliable everblooming qualities, along with the signature flowers.

Also significant in the history of Hybrid Tea roses was the evolution of grafting. Hybrid Tea roses growing on their own roots were not especially vigorous, but by the late 19th century, nursery companies found that these new hybrids grew well when grafted onto the roots of *R. multiflora*. Today, Hybrid Tea roses continue to be grown as grafted plants, with several different rootstocks used.

In the garden, Hybrid Tea roses offer the full range of rose colors, in

Pink-edged 'Garden Party' is a cross of 'Peace' and 'Charlotte Armstrong'.

'Chicago Peace' is a sport of 'Peace' with more copper and orange tones.

'Chrysler Imperial' is known for its shape, color and fragrance.

SOME HIGHLY RATED HYBRID TEAS

'Dainty Bess', 4' x 2'; single, fragrant, pink flowers with showy maroon stamens; thorny. I've found it less susceptible to disease and hardy in Zone 5.

'Fragrant Memory', 5' x 3'; double, high-centered, lavender-pink flowers; Damask fragrance; light green leaves.

'Ingrid Bergman', 3' x 2'; double, high-centered dark red flowers; dark green leaves.

'Mister Lincoln', 5' x 3'; double, quite fragrant, high-centered dark red flowers; dark green, leathery leaves.

'Pink Peace', 5' x 3'; very double, fragrant, high-centered, deep pink flowers; leathery leaves.

'Yves Piaget', 3' x 2'; very double, peony-like, fragrant, pink flowers; deep green leaves.

'Escapade' typifies how Floribundas bloom in clusters.

'Angel Face' is a fragrant Floribunda.

'Touch of Class' is a fragrant Hybrid Tea descended from the Grandiflora 'Queen Elizabeth'.

Polyantha

Late in the 19th century, rose hybridizers made crosses that involved varieties of *R. multiflora*, *R. chinensis*, and the new Hybrid Tea roses. The results were a new class called Polyanthas. These were dainty-looking but tough roses that produced a great number of sprays bearing small flowers. For much of the 20th century, the Polyanthas were often eclipsed in popularity by their flashier cousins, but wise gardeners appreciate them for their attributes: continuous bloom, wide color range and landscape uses.

Polyanthas have narrow, finely textured leaves on the low-growing, bushy plants. Hardy through Zone 5, the plants are excellent for low-maintenance mass plantings, edgings, low hedges and foreground plantings. The sprays of 1-inch, single or semidouble flowers are produced continuously during the growing season. Colors include shades of pink, red, yellow, orange and white. Polyanthas are adaptable to a wide range of soils, but grow their best in rich, moist, but well-drained soil.

mainly semidouble or double form, on narrow, upright bushes growing 3 to 5 feet tall with a small number of stiff stems and and branches. Foliage is large, either shiny or dull green, and sparse, particularly at the base. They are best suited to using in mixed borders or perennial beds.

Most Hybrid Teas are susceptible to insect and disease pests and demand frequent chemical treatments. Most cannot survive without winter protection in Zone 7 and colder. Because of their heavy bloom, they need rich, moist but well-drained soil, with regular fertilizing.

SOME HIGHLY RATED POLYANTHAS

'Cécile Brunner', also known as the "Sweetheart Rose," 3' x 3'; double, high-centered, fragrant, pale pink flowers borne in airy sprays; dark green leaves on slender stems. Besides the climbing form, consider the related 'Spray Cécile Brunner' and 'Perle d'Or'.

'China Doll', 2' x 2'; double pink flowers in large sprays; bright green leaves.

'The Fairy', 2' x 2'; double pink flower; profuse bloomer; glossy, light green leaves; can survive neglect.

'Perfect Moment' is a Hybrid Tea from the German house of Kordes.

A close-up look at the abundant clusters of 'The Fairy'.

Floribunda

As the name implies, Floribundas are noted for their abundance of flowers. Plants bloom repeatedly throughout the growing season, with a stem opening out into a spray of a dozen or more blooms. These flowers may be single, semidouble or double and flat, cupped or high-centered. Bloom size ranges from 2 to 4 inches across, with about every rose color available.

The first Floribundas, 'Else Poulsen' and 'Kirsten Poulsen', were produced in the 1920s by Danish rose breeder Svend Poulsen. Made by crossing Hybrid Tea and Polyantha roses, Floribundas are bushy plants usually growing 2 to 4 feet tall and almost as wide. The plants are widely adapted in the landscape, being useful as specimens in flower beds and borders, as well as planted in masses, or as low hedges or edgings. Most Floribundas are hardy through Zone 6 and withstand colder temperatures with winter protection. They do best with rich, moist but well-drained soil, and regular fertilization.

SOME HIGHLY RATED FLORIBUNDAS

'Betty Prior', 5' x 4'; prolific sprays of single, bright pink flowers; semiglossy leaves.

'Escapade', 3' x 2'; semidouble, flat, fragrant, pink-blend flowers; light to medium green leaves.

'Europeana', 3' x 2'; large sprays of double, velvety red flowers; light fragrance; bronze-green leaves.

'Gene Boerner', 4' x 3'; double, high-centered, pink flowers; medium green, semiglossy leaves.

'Iceberg', 4' x 3'; double, fragrant, white flowers; light green, narrow, glossy leaves.

'Margaret Merril', 2¹/₂' x 2'; small sprays of double, fragrant, blush-white flowers with golden stamens; upright growth; matte, dark green leaves.

'Sunsprite', 3' x 2'; double, fragrant, golden yellow flowers; light green leaves.

Grandiflora

When the Hybrid Teas, with their high-centered flowers and long cutting stems, are crossed with the hardiness, continual flowering and clustered blooms of the Floribundas, the result is the Grandiflora class of roses. This class began with the introduction of 'Queen Elizabeth' in 1954, and she remains the most notable member.

Grandiflora roses are usually the tallest of the Modern Roses, except for Climbers. Generally growing 4 to 6 feet tall, they

'Livin' Easy' was a 1996 AARS winner.

'Cécile Brunner' is a tried-and-true Polyantha.

'Rambling Rector' is a classic, fragrant Rambler.

are striking at the back of beds and borders or as a screening hedge. Grandifloras bloom throughout the growing season, most often in upright sprays with semidouble or double flowers, in all rose colors. They need rich, moist but well-drained, fertile soil. They are hardy through Zone 7, and with winter protection, can survive through Zone 5.

Climber

No rose truly climbs the way plants with tendrils, winding stems or holdfasts do, but a rose can clamber upward with the help of thorns hooking onto tree or shrub branches or man-made supports. With little effort (plus some hand and arm protection), you can attach any rose with long, flexible canes to pillars, posts, fences, trellises or arbors.

Although nearly every classification of roses has some varieties with long canes, in the 20th century a separate class of Large-Flowered Climbing Roses was developed. The heritage of these modern Climbers is derived from a number of different species and Old Garden Roses. Most came from crosses

'Carefree Beauty', a Griffith Buck rose, is one of the modern Shrubs that are so versatile in the garden.

of *R. multiflora* with *R. wichuraiana* (also known as the "Memorial Rose," widely used to decorate tombs), which came from China and has single white flowers on vigorously climbing branches.

Most modern climbing roses grow 6 to 8 feet tall and are

'Queen Elizabeth' reigns supreme among Grandifloras.

Closeup of the fragrant red Rambler 'Chevy Chase', first introduced in 1939.

'El Capitan' shows a typical Grandiflora display.

'Dorothy Perkins' is a familiar Rambler.

SOME HIGHLY RATED CLIMBERS

'Altissimo', 10' x 6'; single, repeat-blooming, velvety red flowers; lightly fragrant; dark green leaves.

'America', 8' x 5'; double, fragrant, repeat-blooming, coral-pink flowers; medium green leaves.

'City of York', 15' x 10'; semi-double, fragrant, once-blooming, creamy white flowers; shiny, leathery leaves.

'Compassion', 10' x 6'; double, fragrant, repeat-blooming, salmon-pink flowers shaded apricot; dark green leaves.

'Handel', 15' x 10'; double, repeat-blooming, deep rose-pink flowers edged in ivory; olive green leaves.

'New Dawn', 15' x 10'; double, fragrant, repeat-blooming, pale pink flowers age to white; small, glossy, dark green leaves.

hardy through Zone 5. The clusters of flowers tend to be similar to Hybrid Teas in appearance. Most bloom repeatedly throughout the growing season, flowering on wood produced in the same season, but a few bloom only once.

Besides the climbing sports of bush roses and the climbing types in all the other categories, especially the Kordes, consider growing Large-Flowered Climbing Roses.

Rambler

Few plants can compete with Rambler roses when they bloom once in early- to midsummer, for the flowers seem to cover every inch. The pliable canes—8 to 20 feet long, sometimes even longer—can be trained onto a pillar, arch, pergola or fence, or be allowed to scramble up into a small tree. The flowers, from 1 to 3 inches across, are produced in large

'Prairie Joy', another tough Buck introduction.

clusters on the new growth. The vigor and hardiness (Zone 5) of Rambler roses is proven by their survival in old cemeteries and abandoned homesteads. In bloom, nothing is so stunning.

Rambler roses were mainly bred in the late 19th and early 20th centuries utilizing

'Prairie Princess' is a hardy, disease-resistant Shrub.

'Ballerina' is a highly rated Hybrid Musk.

'Graham Thomas' is one of the David Austin English Roses that have revolutionized today's gardens.

SOME HIGHLY RATED RAMBLERS

'Albéric Barbier', 20' x 15'; double, creamy white flowers; green apple fragrance; glossy, dark green leaves.

'Chevy Chase', 15' x 12'; double, fragrant, dark crimson-red flowers; soft, light green, wrinkled leaves.

'Hiawatha', 15' x 12'; single, deep pink to crimson flowers with pale centers; light green leaves.

'May Queen', 25' x 15'; very double, quartered, fragrant, pink flowers; occasionally repeat blooms.

'Rambling Rector', 20' x 15'; semidouble, fragrant, creamy to white flowers with yellow stamens; small, gray-green, downy leaves; hips in autumn.

'Tausendschön', 12' x 8'; double, once-blooming, pink flowers with white centers; medium green leaves; nearly thornless.

'Veilchenblau', 15' x 12'; semidouble, fragrant, unusual lavender-purple flowers with white centers and yellow stamens; glossy, light green leaves; nearly thornless.

'American Beauty' is known more for its value as a cut flower than as a garden plant.

AMERICAN BEAUTY: WHAT'S IN A NAME?

If we think that our age has cornered the market on merchandising, we'd be surprised at some of the tactics of our forefathers. One of the most popular roses around, 'American Beauty', enjoys the prestige of connoisseurs because of a savvy marketing ploy.

First, let me give credit to a wonderful author and researcher, Tom Christopher. His *In Search of Lost Roses* (Summit Books, 1989) makes wonderful reading for any gardener, especially rose gardeners. In his book, he outlines the story of the real 'American Beauty'.

A Hybrid Perpetual that debuted in 1875, 'American Beauty' is also called the "Florist's Rose" for its popularity as a long-lasting, long-stemmed red rose that's great for cutting. But in 1875 it was introduced as 'Madame Ferdinand Jamin' by its breeder, a Frenchman named Lédéchaux.

It proved to be hard to grow, and didn't do well in Europe. Entrepreneurial breeders brought it across the Atlantic, where the Baltimore firm of Field Bros. dubbed it with the good old patriotic name 'American Beauty'. It became so popular as a cut flower for one's sweetheart that it revolutionized the floral trade. We buy millions every year.

It also spawned a number of spin-off products that bore the same name, in the hope of riding the patriotic—and successful—wave left by the name. The District of Columbia even adopted it as its official flower.

Still hard to grow for the home gardener, 'American Beauty' is a perfect example of Shakespeare's notion that a rose by any other name would be as sweet—but in this case, it took Yankee ingenuity to make it profitable as well.

'Nevada' has been an excellent Shrub since its introduction in 1927.

R. wichuraiana, R. luciae and *R. multiflora,* along with other species and varieties. There is some discussion among rose experts as to classing some of these as Ramblers or Hybrid Multifloras, but for our purposes they are both included together here.

'Prospero' is a very fragrant English Rose.

'Carefree Delight' is a recently introduced Shrub.

THE LATEST BREAKTHROUGHS

'Othello' (red) and 'Pretty Jessica' show why English Roses are so useful in the landscape.

Introducing Shrub Roses

Take the wealth of genetic material available to rose hybridizers in the 20th century. Combine it with the demand by gardeners for roses that are hardy, adaptable, easy-care, useful throughout the landscape and still beautiful. The result? The large and diverse class of Shrub roses. This class has led the way in changing people's minds about roses, because they've made rose-growing much easier.

Within this catch-all class designated by the American Rose Society are a number of subcategories, some official and others not, that provide a range of plants from groundcovers to giants over 12 feet tall.

Shrub roses have flowers in all rose colors; in singles, semi-doubles and doubles; fragrant or unscented; once- or repeat-blooming. Most varieties are at least hardy through Zone 6, and many are hardy in Zones 4 or 5. A great number also exhibit excellent disease resistance. In the landscape, Shrub roses can be used in mass plantings, hedges, groundcovers, shrub or flower borders or as specimens.

'Pink Bells', a Miniature used as a groundcover.

A mixed rose border: The light pink Climber 'Fantin-Latour' with the English Rose 'Mary Rose' (foreground) and the China 'Gloire des Rosomanes', also known as "Ragged Robin."

Among the officially designated subclasses of Shrub Roses are:

Hybrid Moyesii

The Species *R. moyesii* was brought to the West from China at the turn of the 20th century. It offers deep crimson flowers, dark-green leaves, and bears a great number of large, pendulous, flagon-shaped, orange-red hips. Cultivars may have single or semi-double, red, orange, pink or white, 2-inch flowers that bloom once or repeatedly. Hybrids do not always bear the distinctive hips. These disease-resistant plants form stiff, open shrubs growing 8 to 10 feet tall and just as wide. They are hardy through Zones 4 or 5.

SOME HIGHLY RATED HYBRID MOYESIIS

'Eddie's Jewel', 8' x 6'; double, repeat-blooming, bright red flowers; seldom fruits; few thorns; red bark; Zone 4.

'Geranium', 8' x 5'; single, once-blooming, scarlet flowers in clusters; crimson hips; light green leaves and pale stems; Zone 4.

'Nevada', 8' x 8'; pink buds open to single, repeat-blooming, white flowers; light green leaves and dark brown stems; few thorns; Zone 5.

Hybrid Musk

The namesake of this class, *R. moschata*, is seldom grown, often mislabeled, and at times considered extinct. Native to southern Europe and the Middle East, it is a short climbing rose with gray-green stems and leaves. The white flowers are produced in clusters from mid- to late summer. Significant as the father to the Noisettes, the Musk Rose was part of much breeding work done at the beginning of the 20th century. The resulting class, the Hybrid Musks, have Multiflora roses, Ramblers, Polyanthas, Noisettes, Teas and Hybrid Teas in their heritage.

'Red Meidiland', one of the versatile, tough Meidilands.

'Simplicity', a Floribunda, makes a great hedge.

Graceful plants, the Hybrid Musks are best used in shrub and flower borders, as hedges and as specimen plants. Most grow 5 to 6 feet tall and repeatedly bear large sprays of small, fragrant flowers in soft, delicate colors. They need rich, moist, but well-drained soil and are hardy through Zone 6.

Hybrid Rugosa

Because of their rough, wrinkled leaves and clove-scented flowers, the Rugosa roses are among the easiest to recognize. They are also among the easiest

'Dortmund' is one of the finest roses for pillars or arches. It will bloom all summer long.

of roses to grow, due to their disease-resistant foliage, ability to survive the poor, dry soil of seaside and roadside conditions, and hardiness—in some cases to Zone 2.

Derived from *R. rugosa*, a native of Asia, Hybrid Rugosas usually grow 3 to 6 feet tall and at least 4 feet wide. Plants grown on their own roots will spread by suckers. The repeat-blooming flowers, borne in small clusters, may be single, semidouble or double, in shades of pale to bright pink-red, purple, white or yellow; and accented by golden stamens. Plants bear large red or orange hips in the autumn. Hybrid Rugosas can be used in beds and borders or as specimen plants. They are especially good for hedges, doubly so because of their prickly stems.

Kordesii

Among the most hardy and disease-resistant roses developed in the 20th century are those of the German father-and-son team of Wilhelm and Reimer Kordes.

Most Kordesii varieties are hardy through Zone 4 and withstand a wide range of growing conditions. They enjoy a range of plant sizes and shapes, with most grown as large shrubs or Climbers. Flowers may be single, semidouble or double, come in most rose colors and are once- or repeat-blooming.

Other Shrub roses are available in categories that have become important commercially. These include the following:

'Graham Thomas' (right) in a modern, informal garden setting.

Polyanthas, while others are more shrubby. They generally range from 3 to 5 feet tall. The flowers may be single, semidouble or double, and come in most rose colors.

'Bonica' or "Bonica 82" is a famous modern Shrub from the House of Meilland.

which means they're also disease-resistant. Their appearance is usually between that of Shrub and Floribunda Roses, and plants bloom repeatedly during the growing season. Plant size and flower color and form vary.

Consider any "Parkland" or "Explorer" series roses, as well as those listed below.

SOME HIGHLY RATED KORDESIIS

'Alchymist', 12' x 8'; double, fragrant, once-blooming, apricot-blend flowers; glossy, dark green leaves; stiff, thorny canes; use as a climber; Zone 5.

'Cerise Bouquet', 12' x 12'; pendulous clusters of semidouble, fragrant, repeat-blooming, cerise-crimson flowers; small gray-green leaves; upright to arching canes; Zone 4.

'Dortmund', 8' x 6'; single, repeat-blooming, bright red flowers with a white eye and light fragrance; orange hips; glossy, dark green leaves; stiff, thorny canes; very popular for arches and pergolas; Zone 5.

'Parkdirektor Riggers', 10' x 6'; semidouble, repeat-blooming, velvety red flowers in large clusters; light fragrance; glossy, leathery, dark green leaves; Zone 5.

SOME HIGHLY RATED BUCK HYBRIDS

'Applejack', 5' x 3'; semidouble, large, fragrant, repeat-blooming, bright pink flowers marked with red; leathery leaves.

'Carefree Beauty', 6' x 3'; large, semidouble, repeat-blooming, coral-pink flowers; olive green leaves; orange-red hips.

'Folksinger', 5' x 3'; large, double, fragrant, repeat-blooming, yellow-blend flowers; glossy, leathery, copper-green leaves.

'Maytime', 3' x 3'; large, single, fragrant, repeat-blooming, carmine-red to coral flowers with yellow bases; leathery, bronze-green leaves.

'Prairie Heritage', 4' x 3'; large, double, quartered, fragrant, repeat-blooming, peach to coral pink flowers; leathery, dark-green leaves. This is just one of a number of varieties developed by Professor Buck with names beginning with "Prairie."

Buck Hybrids

Dr. Griffith J. Buck, a professor of horticulture at Iowa State University, developed a group of roses that are hardy through Zone 5 and disease-resistant. Some resemble Floribundas and

Canadian Hybrids

Because of harsh northern winters, rose hybridizers in Canada worked to develop cultivars that are hardy in Zones 3 and 4. Although their heritage is varied, many are derived from Kordesii and Rugosa hybrids,

SOME HIGHLY RATED CANADIAN HYBRIDS

'Alexander Mackenzie', 5' x 4'; double, fragrant, deep pink flowers; waxy, dark green leaves; Zone 3.

'Champlain', 3' x 2'; semidouble, velvety, deep-red flowers; small, yellow-green leaves; best on own roots; Zone 4.

'John Cabot', 6' x 4'; clusters of double, medium-red flowers; medium-green leaves; can be grown as a shrub or climber; Zone 3.

'Morden Centennial', 4' x 3'; clusters of double, medium pink flowers; light fragrance; semi-glossy leaves; Zone 3.

'William Baffin', 6' x 4'; large clusters of double, deep pink flowers; glossy leaves; use as a climber; Zone 3.

'Appleblossom' is one of the new Flower Carpet groundcover roses.

English Roses

Of all the roses developed in the late 20th century, the English Roses developed by Great Britain's David Austin have created the most excitement. Austin crossed such old-fashioned roses as the Gallicas, Damasks, Bourbons and Portlands with modern roses like Hybrid Teas, Floribundas and Climbers. The resulting roses have captured the best of both worlds.

The English Roses generally are bushy plants that bloom repeatedly during the growing season yet have the soft colors and intense fragrances reminiscent of old-fashioned roses. Most of the English roses are hardy through Zone 5. They need rich,

'Flower Carpet White', like many groundcover roses, works well in containers.

moist but well-drained soil that is fertilized regularly.

There are dozens of English rose varieties readily available and more new varieties coming out every year.

Meidiland Roses

One of the major rose hybridizing families in France is that of Meilland. Originally well-known for their Hybrid Tea roses after World War II (they bred the renowned 'Peace'), they have recently gained well-deserved fame for their Shrub and groundcover roses. Called Meidilands, these roses are generally hardy to Zone 4, disease-

SOME HIGHLY RATED ENGLISH ROSES

'Belle Story', 3' x 4'; semidouble, fragrant, pale salmon-pink flowers with yellow centers and golden stamens; medium green leaves; few thorns.

'Cottage Rose', 4' x 4'; double, fragrant, warm pink flowers; medium green leaves.

'Constance Spry', 7' x 7'; double, fragrant, once-blooming, soft pink flowers; large leaves; thorny; use as a climber.

'Fair Bianca', 3' x 3'; double, fragrant, white flowers with green button eyes; compact, upright growth; also consider another white, 'Glamis Castle'.

'Graham Thomas', 6' x 5'; double, fragrant, yellow flowers; upright growth with slender stems.

'Heritage', 4' x 4'; double, fragrant, shell-pink; robust and bushy, with strong stems; few thorns.

'Mary Rose', 5' x 5'; double, fragrant, blush pink flowers; compact, upright growth. 'Redoute' is a sport with paler pink flowers.

'The Herbalist', 3' x 3'; semidouble, fragrant, deep pink flowers with golden stamens that resemble 'Apothecary's Rose'; dark green leaves.

'The Pilgrim', 5' x 5'; double, fragrant, yellow flowers; dark green leaves.

'Flower Carpet Pink' makes a low, informal, season-long hedge.

resistant, and adaptable to a wide range of growing situations. The shrub types are excellent for mass plantings and as hedges.

'Flower Carpet White'.

The Meidilands generally have fine-textured, dark green leaves and clusters of small, repeat-blooming flowers in white and shades of pink and red. The flower clusters, when cut, are an instant bouquet.

SOME HIGHLY RATED MEIDILANDS

'Alba Meidiland', 2' x 6'; double, small white flowers; use as a groundcover or in massed plantings.

'Bonica '82', 5' x 4'; semidouble, small pink flowers; orange-red hips; arching shrub.

'Pink Meidiland', 4' x 4'; single, large, deep pink flowers with white eyes; orange-red hips.

'Scarlet Meidiland', 3' x 6'; double, small, scarlet flowers; tolerates some shade; use as a groundcover or in massed plantings.

'White Meidiland', 2' x 5'; large, double white flowers; large, leathery leaves on thick canes.

MINIATURE ROSES MAKE A BIG SPLASH

'Yellow Doll' (forefront) in a mixed border.

In an age when bigger equals better, Miniature roses offer the gardener a delightful change of pace: a variety of exquisite flower forms and colors that are all the more enchanting because of their diminutive size.

Consider all this in one package:

- The charm of the tiny blossoms—often no more than an inch across when fully open, adorning a plant of proportionate size.
- Winter-hardiness and ability to thrive in a variety of growing conditions.
- Recurrent flowering habit in most varieties.
- You can grow them no matter how little space you have.

Snapshot

Miniatures grow from 6 to 18 inches tall (sometimes taller in balmy southern climates). Their blossoms are in scale with the thin canes and the rest of the plant, not disproportionally big-headed like some overbred annuals you find on the market. Most are repeat-blooming, free-flowering, easy to grow and wonderfully versatile.

Miniature roses as a class are quite winter-hardy, the result of being grown on their own roots (except for some of the grafted "standard" Miniatures). And they're not prone to disease or pest damage.

Patio roses are an informal class of Miniatures, considered too large in blossom size and growth habit to be true miniatures, yet smaller than their full-sized counterparts.

Picture a rock garden planted with an assortment of cool, blue-green-leaved perennials and miniature evergreens, bejeweled with apricot 'Loving Touch' or yellow 'Sequoia Gold'. Or an array of hanging baskets planted with pale pink 'Nozomi', offering far more refinement than a basket of petunias could approach. And instead of a low-growing hedge of boxwood around your herb garden, think

'Honey Moss'.

of the color and interest a row of salmon-pink 'Angela Rippon' could provide!

An acquaintance has taken "how to win friends and influence people" to a whole new level. In his garden he grows Miniature rose varieties that assure a continuous supply of blossoms throughout the season. Each morning, he gathers an assortment of mini-rose flowers. As he makes calls on customers and colleagues, he dispenses single buds in tiny bud vases, brightening many a face and desk.

Miniature roses are excellent when cut for arrangements, boutonnieres or bud vases, and also

'Popcorn'.

'Luvvie'.

'Gold Coin', a Ralph Moore introduction.

are great for drying. There are even climbing Miniatures.

A Tiny Bit of History

Miniature roses are not the result of trimming the roots of full-size plants or of drastic pruning. Rather, they're the result of hybridization—crossing full-size roses of many classes, such as Hybrid Teas and Rugosas, with roses that have been developed from the original Miniature rose, *Rosa chinensis minima*.

Although the history is sometimes hazy, it goes like this:

R. chinensis minima was introduced to Europe from China in the early 1800s. As its name implies, *minima* is a dwarf of *Rosa*

Miniatures like 'Starina' have opened up new possibilities for all gardeners.

'Woman's Day'.

chinensis or "China Rose," and it carries the China's repeat-blooming habit. Most important for breeders, this trait is dominant when *minima* is cross-bred with other roses—it will miniaturize larger roses.

One of these "fairy roses," 'Pompon de Paris', was a popular potted plant, sold in the street markets of Paris in the 1830s and 1840s. However, other roses became fashionable in Victorian times and Miniatures eventually fell out of favor. A standard rose text of 1930 does not mention Miniatures at all.

Around 1917, a Swiss army medical officer named Colonel Roulet discovered a small rose, perfect in proportion, growing on a window ledge in a town in the Swiss Alps. This rose was described as being only 5 or 6 inches tall, with deep pink flowers less than half an inch across. It was named in his honor, *R. rouletti* (now recognized as a hybrid named 'Rouletti').

A Dutchman, Jan de Vink, and a Spaniard, Pedro Dot, advanced Miniature breeding into a new era. The Dutchman developed an important and successful diminutive rose, introduced to commerce in 1936, known as 'Peon'. It has red flowers with a white eye. When Robert Pyle (of the 100-year-old American rose house Conard-Pyle) marketed 'Peon' as 'Tom Thumb', Miniatures took off in America.

Dot discovered the dominant dwarfing trait, which opened the door to hybridizing Minis with just about every rose imaginable. He was the first breeder to add yellow to the Miniatures palette in 1940 with 'Baby Gold Star'.

A legendary American rose hybridizer, Californian

'Honest Abe'.

'Holy Toledo'.

Ralph Moore, is responsible for many of the beautiful Miniatures available to us today. Beginning in the 1930s, Moore developed the first American-bred Miniatures, including 'Cutie', introduced in 1952, and since then has bred varieties with a vast variety of flower form and color, including 'Rise 'n' Shine', 'Easter Morn', 'Happy Thought' and 'Stars 'n' Stripes'.

'Popcorn' in a patio setting.

'Bambino' (orange-red) used in a classic cottage garden setting.

CHAPTER 4

ROSES IN THE LANDSCAPE: THE NEW LOOK

Landscaping with roses is largely a matter of planting them where they'll give you the most satisfaction. Maximum rose enjoyment means dealing with several factors: your available planting sites, your choice of roses and your dreams as a gardener. Do you want to have fragrant roses to share with friends, or to show off when they come over? Accent a nice-looking corner of your property, or cover up an eyesore? In this chapter we explore basic requirements that must be met for your roses to flourish. Then we show you 11 very different ways that versatile roses may be used to enrich your home landscape with their beauty, fragrance and eye appeal.

Since roses often look best when grown in the company of other flowers, we also introduce a wide selection of annuals, perennials and groundcover plants that make fine companions for roses. And, since many roses demand open space where they can bask in fresh air and sunshine, we also discuss lawns and hard surfaces in some detail.

After a season or two, you may find that certain cultivars show uncharacteristic growth habits when you grow them in your yard. Perhaps an English rose insists on growing into a tall pillar, or a Miniature shows a strong inclination to sprawl. One of the secrets of landscaping with roses is making the most of these kinds of surprises. When landscaping with roses, flexibility is as important to your success as thoughtful planning.

ANALYZING YOUR SITE

To evaluate potential planting places for your roses, begin by learning the directional orientation of your yard. If you don't know what it is, you can use a compass to find your property's north-south axis, or use the sun as your guide. The sun's actual angle varies with the seasons. In summer the points where the sun rises and sets shift toward the north. In winter they shift toward the south.

Armed with this basic information about exposure, you can clearly identify patterns of light and wind in your yard. In all climates, roses require at least six hours of direct sun each day, plus plenty of fresh air to circulate through the leaves. Morning sun is especially beneficial since it helps dew to dry quickly, thus discouraging black spot and other fungal diseases that spread when leaves are

Happy marriages of flower forms and varieties aren't an accident. The most enjoyable gardens result when the gardener studies the site first.

wet. In different climates, certain special exposures (described in the "Climate Matters" box below) are well worth pursuing.

Drainage

Low spots where puddles form and persist for more than a few hours after a heavy rain are not suitable for roses. Your plants will get root rot or other diseases. Certain selections may tolerate damp conditions for a short period of time, but they'll grow much better when planted where the soil is well drained. Improving the soil's texture before planting (as described in Chapter 5) also will improve its drainage, but no amount of soil amendments will correct a drainage problem that's caused by inadequate slope or other gross imperfections in the site. If every available place in your yard has questionable drainage, you'll need to grow roses in raised beds or containers.

CLIMATE MATTERS

• In cool climates where there is persistent fog or cloud cover, roses generally require full sun. When they must be grown near houses or large trees, place them on the south side where sunlight is most abundant.
• Where summers are warm and dry, many roses grow well with six hours of direct sun each day. Filtered afternoon shade that reduces the plants'

needs for water may actually be beneficial.
• In humid climates, roses benefit greatly from full morning sun. They also need wide spacing to facilitate good air circulation.
• Where winds are persistent and strong, reduce the wind's force by planting roses where they will receive some protection by way of a low wall, open fence or hedge of shrubs.

An overflowing 'Paul's Scarlet Climber' is stunning outside a dining room window, and can be enjoyed from inside the house as well.

Traffic Patterns and Boundaries

Since roses are prickly plants, they must be located a few feet away from walkways and areas where people get in and out of cars, and you certainly would not want to place roses adjacent to where children romp and play. In any yard, there are probably natural pathways that people and pets use over and over again. Placing roses so that they become obstacles to natural traffic patterns is asking for trouble (unless you want to eliminate such traffic).

At the same time, you need to be able to reach all parts of your roses easily, to gather cut blossoms and check them often for evidence of pests or disease. The roses you choose especially for their fragrance are best placed near areas where you like to relax. Better yet, locate them where you can sink your nose into their perfumed blossoms.

The thorns that make roses unsuitable in close quarters make them ideal for defining boundaries. Roses are naturals as living fences, intermittent hedges or centerpiece specimen plants in beds located to mark your garden's edge. As long as light and fresh air are abundant, you can train climbers onto fences, or you might train lanky roses into upright pillars to serve as visual markers for an otherwise undefined edge.

Put It on Paper

At this point it is wise to record on paper what you know about your site and its suitability for roses. Make a rough drawing of your yard (graph paper is good for this), and draw in "bubbles" where spots seem promising for roses. These areas may be circular, oblong or even dog-legged in shape. Avoid using only squares and rectangles.

Baby's breath and lavender frame the focal point created by a standard rose.

With drawing in hand, go inside your house and try to imagine how those spaces will look from inside after they're teeming with roses. Since roses are natural focal points, strive to locate them where you can enjoy them from as many vantage points as possible, indoors and out.

You can create vertical focal points and control the traffic flow within your garden with roses on arches.

SWEET SPOTS FOR ROSES

• Any high spot that drains very quickly and gets lots of sunshine and fresh air (all roses).
• The top of a retaining wall backfilled with good soil (Grandifloras, Hybrid Teas).
• The high edge of a brick or stone patio (Miniatures).
• A brick wall that faces south or southeast (Climbers).
• An eye-catching island in a sea of green lawn (Floribundas, showy Shrub roses).
• Large containers placed in full morning sun (small Floribundas, Miniatures).
• A gentle slope that faces south or southeast (spreading landscape roses).
• Boundaries in full sun (many Old Roses, Species, Shrub roses, Rugosas).

VISUAL FRAMES

Mulches and hedges—this one is boxwood —provide great frames for roses.

Just as a painting does not appear complete until it is framed and hung, roses look best when their planting place includes some sort of visual frame. As you look at the pictures throughout this book, notice how the most attractive plantings are flanked by plants, paving or fine-texture mulch. Sometimes called neutral zones, the visual frames you choose will depend on your site, the style of your garden, and how much money and mainte-nance you are willing to invest.

The Lawn

A well-kept lawn makes everything around it look bet-ter, including roses. A lawn need not be large to be effec-tive. Swaths of healthy grass only a few feet square bring a vibrant green color and fine texture to the garden, both of which are flattering to roses. A high-quality lawn separated from a bed of roses by a brick

mowing strip is visu-ally pleasing and easy to maintain.

Hard Surfaces

Any garden struc-ture made from stone, brick or con-crete is called a hard surface. The textures of hard surfaces con-trast beautifully with plants, and also pro-vide an element of continuity within the garden. Low stone or brick walls can help stabilize slopes while creating planting pockets for roses and other plants. Hard-surfaced patios and walkways create clean floors for outdoor activi-ties, and require less mainte-nance than lawns.

Carefully consider drainage when adding patios or hard-sur-faced walkways to your land-scape. Since rainwater runs over hard surfaces rather than perco-lating through them, areas at the low end of any hard surface tend to collect moisture. If this is like-ly to be a problem, a series of steppingstones may be a better alternative.

Mulches

Attractive mulches help plants grow better by retaining soil moisture. They also enrich the garden with their color and texture. In areas where pine needles are abundant, they make a pretty mulch suitable for both plants and pathways. You also can use shredded bark, pebbles or other materials. To help keep weeds from invading large mulched areas, place per-forated black plastic or some type of landscape fabric beneath

'Summer Fashion' softens a hard-edged patio and wall.

the mulch. If you grow many plants in containers, mulching the "floor" of your garden is especially useful.

Edging Plants

When planted as edgings around rose beds, plants can be used to create a visual frame. From Zone 6 southward, *Liriope muscari* is widely used for this purpose. *Liriope spicata* is hardy to Zone 4. Evergreen candytuft (hardy to Zone 4) requires more maintenance, but it also makes a fine edging plant. To edge beds, you also can use small annuals, including alyssum, lobelia or nemophilia. Gray-foliage plants such as stachys (lamb's-ear), dusty miller and santolina are always welcome at the garden's edge.

A simple brick edging can separate your rose beds from the lawn and protect plants from the mower.

SMART LANDSCAPING STRATEGIES

Curved, mixed beds featuring roses create an informal style.

If you think of your landscape as a room, with a floor, ceiling and walls, it may be easier to decide where to place roses. Review this checklist while sitting in the general area where you hope to plant your roses, and use these ideas to envision your yard as a furnished outdoor room.

1. Stick with a Style

If your personal tastes run toward things that are very neat and orderly, you may be happiest with a formal style. Formal gardens are usually structured with straight lines, and are symmetrical in their overall design. Informal gardens are structured with curves, and rely on balance rather than symmetry to make them feel unified and whole.

These variegated irises mix well with lighter-colored roses and cover the stems.

'Iceberg' as a focus in a more formal bed, nicely set off by the brick-edged green lawn.

2. Build Up a Backdrop

At least one "wall" of your landscape should have a strong structure that makes it work as a backdrop. Natural backdrops include shrub borders or woodland areas. Fences or tall hedges may be added to a plain landscape to make it feel more lush and cozy.

3. Enhance a Focal Point

Look for an area of your yard that is sunny and well drained, and would become an instant destination if planted with roses. Consider how you might connect this place to the house with a walkway or series of stepping-stones. You can use statuary, birdbaths or garden ornaments to further define a focal point.

4. Screen Unwanted Views

If you discover things you'd rather not see, imagine ways you might block these items from view with trees, a panel of attractive wood fence or perhaps a grouping of evergreens or shrubs. Avoid planting roses or other showy plants where they will call attention to things you would prefer to hide from view.

5. Create Vertical Interest

Landscape features that rise up vertically bring drama to the garden while creating a feeling of enclosure. Large climbing roses

are unsurpassed for use as pillars or walls that help turn a yard into a beautiful outdoor room.

6. Add Accessories

If your yard is small or includes a number of stocky trees, imagine how you might use plants grown in containers or small beds to embellish your landscape without overpowering it. Perhaps a comfortable bench could face a trio of fragrant roses. Or a large wooden box planted with Miniatures might be the ideal way to accessorize your deck.

Foliage contrast is another eye-pleaser. Here, 'Zéphirine Drouhin' with artemisia 'Silver King' make an ordinary fence look special.

Mixed borders with straight lines outlined by a boxwood hedge.

COLOR AND FORM

Single-color plantings can be relaxing settings, especially when complemented by neutral tones of benches, paving and urns.

The artistic side of gardening should be an ongoing source of fun, for choosing colors is not very complicated, and there are few absolute rights and wrongs. In rose gardening, you can begin with whatever selections interest you most, and use those blossom colors as a starting point. Better yet, study the landscape itself before deciding which colors will work best for you.

Instead of becoming preoccupied with colors that match, base most of your decisions about color on the idea of *contrast*. For example, dark-colored roses show off best when grown against a light background, which explains the heavy use of white picket fences and white trellises with bright red roses. The same setting would make light colored roses look lost and pale. To make the most of possible contrast, it would be much better to locate a pastel rose

against a backdrop of dark evergreens, or perhaps a dark-colored part of your house or fence.

Moody Hues

Colors also help set the mood in the garden. Cool colors, including white and pastel shades of pink and blue, tend to feel relaxing. They are best used in close quarters, for they have very little impact when viewed from a distance. Red and orange are hot colors that naturally create excitement. These are high-impact colors, easily seen from afar, that create a mood of happy exuberance.

Adding Neutrals

The factors that you must consider when choosing roses may limit you to a few selections that could possibly clash if they came into bloom at the same

time. Some gardeners solve this by establishing separate beds for different color schemes. Where this isn't practical, allow as much space as possible between orange and pink roses (a natural clash), and fill the buffer zone with plants and flowers that provide such neutral tones as white, pale yellow or gray. Many of the companion plants featured in the following pages have been chosen because of their ability to neutralize potential color discord in the garden.

Natural Complements

When it comes to color, opposites attract. This is another way of saying that colors that are radically different from one another often look wonderful together. For example, orange looks great with blue, and violet sings alongside chartreuse. You can discover other opposites like this (called complementary colors) by look-

Orange-toned roses can either shock the eye or provide pleasing contrast, depending on the company they keep.

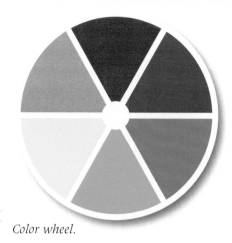

Color wheel.

ing at the color wheel above. To find three-way matches (called split complements), rotate a small triangle in the middle of the wheel. The points of the triangle will point to three colors that will work together.

Adding Evergreens

Green is definitely a color to consider when landscaping with roses, for few roses are a good source of vibrant green color. Roses also are deciduous in most climates, and there is certainly nothing attractive about a rose bound up in burlap for the winter. Strategic placement of evergreens helps infuse the rose garden with greenery in summer, and makes it look less like a graveyard in winter. Where protection is needed from persistent

Lighter-colored roses are set off by trees, hedges and evergreens.

frigid winds, low-growing junipers and other hardy evergreens also may be planted on the north side of exposed roses to form a sheltered windbreak.

Fresh Forms

The notion that opposite colors attract applies to the subject of form—both the forms of flowers and the forms of the plants themselves. Roses, for the most part, are either angular upright bushes, loose fountains of arching canes, or leggy climbers. Therefore they tend to look best in the company of plants with different forms, such as low, mounding plants, vertical upright spikes, or any plants with a very soft, airy texture. One thing roses aren't is soft and airy.

No other flower blossoms look like roses, so it's an easy task to find companion plants that provide a contrast in flower form. Daisies, coreopsis and other flowers with flat, open blossoms look great with roses, as do flowers that develop tall spikes, such as larkspur and mealycup sage.

Good Company

The best companion plants for roses have several things in common. Above the ground, they are small plants that do not block the sunshine and fresh air that roses require. Below ground, they have shallow or skimpy root systems that do not pose serious competition for nutrients and moisture. Still, when using any companion plants with roses, it is best to grow them in "planting pockets" maintained just outside the root zones of your roses.

Many of the most desirable companion plants are annuals that are pulled up in the fall and replanted anew in spring. This seasonal renovation simplifies off-season rose care chores, such as replacing mulch, pruning and dormant spraying. Numerous dwarf annuals work well with

Evergreen shrubs provide a backdrop to this arbor-trained 'American Pillar'.

roses, but let your climate govern your final choices. Pansies, for example, bloom prolifically all summer in the North, but die out in June in the South. Heat-loving ageratum, on the other hand, thrives in humid heat, yet struggles to survive where nights are cool. In the landscaping schemes that follow, widely adapted companion plants are named in special sections called "Good Company." You'll find more details on the most widely used plants in the "Gallery of Companion Plants" that begins on page 82. Use these plants as a starting point for selecting colorful partners for your roses!

*Lupines and foxgloves (*Digitalis *spp.) complement bright pink roses.*

COURTYARD COMPANY

We use courtyards and patios because they offer us privacy, and a chance to make our own outdoor living space. Roses have been grown in these settings for centuries as specimens or as relaxed landscape accents.

Roses have much to offer in the enclosed space of an intimate courtyard or patio garden, where each of their attributes seems more focused and finely honed. Fragrances seem sharper, colors clearer and forms more defined when you use roses as feature plants in open-air outdoor rooms. Since many centuries-old roses were selected and bred to grow in the courtyard gardens of castles and monasteries, it can be argued that growing roses in modern patio gardens is simply an update of a very old idea.

Because walls are such an important part of a courtyard garden, finding a good place for a pretty climbing rose is a logical first step for any lover of roses.

Also keep in mind that when large vertical plants are added to small landscapes, they automatically become important structural elements.

When landscaping within a space that is already well defined as an outdoor room, the concept of scale is a useful guideline. Avoid using huge plants that will make everything near them look small. When you use a medium-large plant like a climbing rose, balance it with a different plant of similar size and mass. For example, you might balance a single robust Climber placed in a warm, sunny spot with a small ornamental tree in the opposite sector of the garden.

Roses in Outdoor Rooms

Most patio gardens are heavily used for outdoor dining and relaxing, and include a large concrete, brick or stone surface just outside the door. If you do a lot of entertaining, a small section of lawn next to the patio will provide needed overflow space for guests and help frame a pretty bed of roses just beyond. If you were to place your roses right along the edge of the paved "floor," they might

An informal sitting area with Hybrid Rugosa 'Sir Thomas Lipton' in front, and the modern Shrub 'Carefree Beauty' against the rear wall.

become an unwelcome or even dangerous barrier.

Early on, decide where you will place a table and chairs, and then look for a spot for a high-visibility rose bed. If the garden is a straight-sided square or rectangle, a centrally located circular bed will be an elegant feature that unifies the landscape like magic. Within a focal-point bed, you might plant a single large Grandiflora surrounded by Miniatures and companion plants with showy foliage. Or you might use the space for a small water feature, and flank it with light-colored roses that are easily seen at night.

Any bed that adjoins a hard surface should be framed with brick, stone or landscaping timbers to slightly raise it above the level of the surrounding patio. Besides improving drainage,

A simple path leading to a shed can be dressed up with accent roses.

Climbing 'Cécile Brunner' helps make this outdoor room into a haven.

Delizy') and little Polyanthas (e.g., 'The Fairy'). You can keep these container-grown plants in a seldom-seen area, and move them to the patio when they bloom. Place very fragrant selections on platforms or tables to bring them close to nose level.

Good Company

In any garden where hard surfaces are extensively used, soft-textured plants provide beautiful contrast. Use annuals that produce sprays of tiny flowers that give them a cloud-like appearance, such as annual baby's breath or sweet alyssum. Spreading thymes form puffy pillows of fragrant foliage that are perfect for softening the edges of angular beds. Velvety silver lamb's ear or dusty miller marry beautifully with stone; 'Bath's Pink' dianthus brings the extra bonus of fragrant pink flowers in early spring.

raising and enclosing the planting space will stop soil from washing out, and make it possible to sweep the area clean quickly.

Potted Accents

If the corners of the garden offer enough sun, they may be ideal spots for roses in containers. Choose broad containers that are not easily toppled and which have several drainage holes in the bottom. Plant them with small bushy roses or Miniatures, and add a few dainty cascading annuals. For example, petunias, sweet alyssum and lobelia will gradually spill over the edges of the pots, which will help the containers look attractive even when the roses aren't in bloom.

A sunny porch or patio is also a great place to display very fragrant roses grown in containers. If there is another part of your yard that gets good sun, perhaps you can use it as a nursery area for fragrant Old Roses that grow well in containers. Several classes have numerous good candidates, especially antique Tea roses (for example, the sunset-toned 'Rosette

Such gray accent plants as artemisias set off pink roses well.

FRAGRANT FRIENDS

All the roses in a courtyard garden need not be fragrant, but try to include at least two selections with strong, clean noses such as 'Starina' (orange-red Miniature), 'Jardins de Bagatelle' (pink Grandiflora), 'Iceberg' (white Floribunda), 'Zéphirine Drouhin' (pink Climber), and numerous Hybrid Teas and Old Roses.

Scented geraniums (*Pelargonium* spp.), which are usually grown in pots, release their scents when gently brushed. Keep a few pots of rose-, apple-, or mint-scented geranium on your deck or patio to provide fragrance when your roses are not in bloom.

Courtyard or patio gardens are more intimate living settings. Here we can concentrate on our roses' most enjoyable features, for example, their petal form or fragrance.

A ROSE CUTTING GARDEN

Creating a rose garden that produces an abundance of blooms to use in arrangements is much simpler today than in times past, thanks in large part to the development of new rose cultivars. Until the 1980s, only Hybrid Teas were thought worthy of inclusion in rose cutting gardens, because of the beauty of their blooms and their strong repeat blooming habit. Today many other roses share these characteristics, including English, Shrub and landscaping roses.

In order for roses to produce high-quality blooms over an extended season, they require an excellent site, meticulous care and a certain sensitivity to how each individual variety or cultivar adapts to its environment. For this reason, a roses-only bed in a very sunny, well-drained site is usually a cornerstone in a rose cutting garden. Within the bed, roses may be arranged according to their heights, with tall Grandifloras and pillars in the rear, bushy cultivars in the center, and

Roses grown for cutting delight visitors young and old.

Miniatures or angular Hybrid Teas in the foreground.

Give the plants plenty of space so you can easily access every side with your pruning shears, and strategically place steppingstones inside the bed so you'll have a place to stand and work. Grow companion plants to use in arrangements in other parts of the landscape.

Diversify the types of roses grown, for cutting naturally provides you with opportunities to create different types of arrangements. For example, you might display single buds or blossoms of Hybrid Teas or Grandifloras in a simple crystal vase, and make an informal composition that uses other summer flowers with multi-flowered stems from Floribundas. English roses often must be

Floribundas such as 'Sexy Rexy' are great plants for a cutting garden.

TIP

TABLESCAPING WITH ROSES

When choosing roses, emphasize colors that look good in your home. In dim indoor lighting, light-colored roses often look best, including soft peachy pinks. Fragrant roses of any color are always welcome indoors!

taken on rather short stems, which makes them ideal for arranging in small containers ranging from silver pitchers to rustic mugs and simple bowls.

Kindest Cuts

When cutting roses, bear in mind that you are actually pruning the plants. To decide exactly where to cut a Hybrid Tea or other reblooming rose, look for a bud along the stem that faces outward. Next examine the leaflet beneath that bud. If the

GREAT GRANDIFLORAS

Grandiflora roses are best thought of as oversized Hybrid Teas with the vigor and tendency to produce loose clusters of flowers like Floribundas. They are often used as anchor plants in rose cutting gardens. These vigorous cultivars often grow to 6 feet tall, and rebloom constantly all summer when properly fertilized, pruned and deadheaded. Top selections include pink 'Queen Elizabeth' and yellow 'Gold Medal'. For outstanding fragrance, consider deep red 'Love's Promise'.

A cutting garden doesn't have to look like a parade ground.

leaflet has five leaves or more, the bud will probably grow into a new flowering stem. Cut the stem 1/2 inch above this bud.

Take a container of warm water with you when you gather cut roses, and place the stems in the water immediately. When you are finished cutting, sit down with your prun-

TIP **DOUBLE YOUR PLEASURE**

When properly handled, rose blossoms continue to open after they're cut. Because of this, rose blossoms that have numerous petals that unfurl over several days' time usually last longer in a vase than those that produce single flowers.

ing shears and snip off all of the lower leaves that will be submerged once the arrangement is made. After trimming, place the stems in warm water—as hot as your hand can bear—and let them rest in a dark place for a few hours. This conditioning will add several days to their vase life.

Your arrangements will look even better if you take a few minutes to clean and polish the rose foliage as you set each stem in place. Wipe leaves gently with a damp cloth, and then polish them lightly with a dry cloth lubricated with a few drops of vegetable oil.

Finding Local Favorites

Rosarians who grow roses for exhibition prefer plants that produce lovely blossoms and are strong repeat bloomers—the same things flower arrangers are after. Many local and regional rose societies publish lists of these high-performance roses, which is a great starting place for choosing selections for cutting. One easy way to access this information is go to the American Rose Society's Internet site (http://www.ars.org), and connect to the links provided to local rose organizations.

Climbers, such as 'Belle Portugaise', provide buckets of bouquets.

Good Company

Enrich your landscape with plants that provide cutting material that works well with roses. Some good choices include white gypsophila (perennial baby's breath), an easy-to-grow plant that produces long, stiff stems studded with hundreds of tiny white flowers. Russian sage (*Perovskia* spp.) is another good perennial to work into rose arrangements. Also make use of flowering shrubs, including hydrangea and viburnums, as well as variegated groundcover plants such as vinca and variegated English ivy. Cut ferns show off roses well too.

Hybrid Teas 'Chrysler Imperial' (red) and 'Tropicana' (salmon) are excellent cutting specimens.

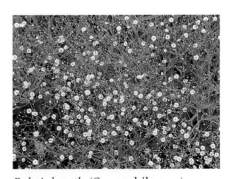

Baby's breath (Gypsophila spp.) accompanies many a bouquet of cut flowers, and it's easy to grow.

DEFINING BOUNDARIES

Hedges made of roses fit any number of outdoor settings. Here the Hybrid Musk 'Ballerina' will give a pool a splash of color all summer long with its blooms.

With or without the stiff backbone of a fence, you can use roses to bring structure and color to the boundaries of your landscape. Boundary plantings create privacy within a yard. When thorny roses are a major component of boundary plantings, they also deter intruders and unwanted foot traffic. At the same time, they're like an open invitation to wild birds, for rose hedges provide birds with cover, protection and food.

You can arrange roses in a solid, unbroken line to form a hedge, or you can space them farther apart so that they form a more undulating silhouette. The latter approach works best with large, sprawling roses since it provides access to the plants on all sides. Smaller cultivars that are more upright work well as continuous hedges.

Adding Structure

Since roses are deciduous plants, you may want to make either a fence or grouping of stalwart evergreen shrubs, planted in a repetitive pattern, part of your boundary grouping. Using a wood, iron or rustic cedar fence gives you a wide choice of styles that can help unify the boundary planting with the rest of your landscape. In landscapes that have a strong formal style, low hedges of clipped boxwood, yew or other evergreens planted parallel to the rose hedge often work well.

"Stone walls do not a prison make," especially when they're softened by such captivating roses as 'Paul's Scarlet Climber'.

Choose the right size Shrub rose to fit the height of a stone wall.

LOW-MAINTENANCE HEDGE ROSES

Zones 4 to 9:

'Carefree Beauty', large pink flowers on shrubby bushes to 6 feet tall; good fall hips.

'Carefree Wonder', medium pink flowers; shrubby bushes to 4 feet tall; heavy flowering.

'Cherry Meidiland', single red blossoms; upright bushes to 4 feet tall.

'Linda Campbell', double red blossoms in clusters; 4 feet tall.

'Royal Bonica', deep pink blossoms in clusters; 4-5 feet tall.

'Scarlet Meidiland', bright scarlet, long-lasting bouquets; nice foliage; 4-5 feet tall.

'The Fairy', clusters of pink blossoms; bushy 3-foot-tall plants; repeats well.

Zones 5 to 9:

'F. J. Grootendorst', clusters of red flowers; prickly 6-foot-tall bush; good hips.

Zones 6 to 9:

'Fair Bianca', double white blooms; compact bushes to 4 feet tall; very fragrant.

'Graham Thomas', yellow cupped blooms; bushy 6-foot plants; fragrant.

'Old Blush', pink blossoms in loose clusters; bushy plants to 5 feet; orange hips.

TIP — OPTICAL ILLUSIONS

A long continuous line of the same kind of plant tends to make the line look longer, while an intermittent hedge appears to shorten the distance from one end to the other. You can accentuate the length of a hedge by planting such evergreen groundcover plants as liriope or pachysandra at its base.

'Mme. Isaac Pereire' reclines on a stone wall and steals the scene.

TIP

BRIGHTS AND WHITES

To turn a plain white picket fence into a vision of beauty, provide it with the happy company of bright red Floribunda roses like 'Europeana' or 'John Franklin'. The crispness of the white fence will set off the red roses like a spotlight. If desired, dress the base of the roses with white narrow-leaf zinnias.

The Large-Flowered Climber 'City of York' is a vigorous plant that can grow 15 feet tall.

'Cécile Brunner' makes a tall iron fence softer to the eye.

When you put roses to work defining boundaries, you'll probably use a number of plants. For this reason alone, it is crucial to choose cultivars that will require little care and grow well in your climate. Even the most rugged roses are not totally maintenance-free. All roses require that you cut out dead canes, remove tree seedlings and other woody weeds that become established in the planting, and perhaps give heavy-duty pruning shears a good workout once or twice a year as you shape the plants. If you're willing to attend to these minimal tasks,

Climbing 'Butterscotch' with a companion of proportionate height, Japanese maple, Acer palmatum.

you can grow a beautiful hedge or screen made of roses.

Closely study the shape of plants you are considering for a hedge. At best, they should be bushy plants that grow 3 to 5 feet tall, and less than 4 feet wide. Roses that grow wider than this form an impenetrable thicket, so they are best used for mass planting on slopes or other inaccessible places (see page 76). Choose shorter roses—less than 4 feet tall—for small properties. Six-foot Rugosas and many other Old Roses are useful for defining the boundaries of larger spaces. Any roses that set a good crop of hips are highly desirable, for they extend the season of interest well into winter.

Finally, take no chances with winter hardiness when choosing roses for planting as a living

An airy split rail fence fills in when a bushy rose ('Mrs. Sam McGredy') grows through it.

Pachysandra and other groundcovers are better companions than grass. They add texture and color, and never need mowing.

fence. Hedge roses always should be grown on their own roots, with hardiness ratings that meet or exceed the demands of your climate. Some of the best cultivars for hedges are summarized on page 64.

Good Company

Frequently nothing is needed at the base of a hedge, for keeping the surrounding area in lawn usually makes a hedge appear neat and well maintained. If you use roses that grow into open, fountain-shaped plants in an intermittent hedge, flank them with groundcover plants that do not require mowing, such as pachysandra. Mowing around and beneath long, thorny canes is often painful or impossible.

'Buff Beauty', a Hybrid Musk, is a good trellis rose.

FANCIFUL FOUNDATIONS

The practice of dressing the base of buildings with shrubs, called foundation plantings, developed primarily in response to the proliferation of ranch-style or "rambler" houses. The tremendously functional interior floor plans of ranch houses of the '50s and '60s left much to be desired on the outside. Architects and landscape designers found a solution by adapting a practice once reserved only for grand houses—softening the boxy lines of homes with shrubs to make them look taller, broader and more appealing to the eye.

Today, foundation plantings are incorporated into all landscapes, regardless of architectural style. Foundation shrubs are mostly evergreens, for only evergreens can mask the base of a house year round. Yet deciduous shrubs like roses also have a place in foundation plantings. They are especially useful for filling foundation areas that you want to remain somewhat open, such as the spot in front of a basement window or crawl space vent. You also can use them to add depth to shrub groupings that are comprised mostly of evergreens.

The front yards of many homes include a walkway down one side of the house that leads from the driveway or parking area to the front door. In the interest of safety, avoid crowding plants that might become obstacles near the walkway. Instead, extend the foundation plantings on the opposite, open side of the house forward so that it becomes a deep bed. The edge of this bed may be a straight line, parallel to the house, or you can make it more dramatic by shaping it into a broad curve. Use roses and other color plants in the foreground of this bed, and then add a neat edging to separate it from the lawn.

 SMALL YARD STRATEGY

In keeping with the small scale of a tiny yard, you can put Miniatures to work in a foundation planting. Plant them in a rhythmic pattern with neat dwarf evergreens such as edging boxwoods and small drifts of daffodils or other spring-blooming bulbs. Or grow Miniatures in roomy window boxes above dwarf evergreen shrubs.

The Climber 'Handel' combines with lavender, lilies and other roses to give eye appeal to the front of this house.

TIP

GOOD COMPANY

Use colorful edging plants to help define the transition between the lawn and foundation shrubs. Shallow-rooted annuals like dwarf snapdragons often work well, or you can use very compact shrubs such as dwarf nandina (Zones 7 to 9). Dwarf 'Sunny' dahlias are another prime possiblity for foundation beds.

Practical Matters

Light exposure may limit the sites that can support roses, as well as the growth habits of the roses themselves. If your house faces north, for example, there might not be enough sun to support roses. However, houses that face southeast or southwest usually can accommodate roses grown as part of a front yard foundation grouping.

COMELY MULCHES

More than any other plants in your landscape, foundation shrubs of all types need a hard-working and attractive mulch. The eaves of a house divert rainfall and reduce the amount of water that reaches foundation beds, which increases the need for a moisture-retentive mulch. Mulches also keep muddy water from staining the side of your house, help with weed and disease control, and give the foundation bed a neat, well-groomed appearance. You can use any type of mulch in a foundation bed, including shredded bark, pine needles, pebbles and marble chips. Just keep in mind that in this landscaping situation, looks are just as important as function. (See the full section on Mulch on pp. 112-113.)

All foundation shrubs, including roses, should never be allowed to crowd windows. Overgrown shrubs that cannot be tamed by pruning deserve total removal, which may open up a perfect spot for a drift of roses. When planting roses near windows, choose selections whose mature heights match those of the window's ledge. Also, plant them two to three feet away from the wall of the house. This way, the plants will enjoy good air circulation and you will be able to see them easily when looking out the window. Overhanging eaves with gutters also tend to reduce the amount of water that reaches plants set close to the exterior wall, which is another reason to leave a 3-foot margin between the wall and foundation shrubs.

Color and Form

Any rose will become an instant focal point when grown in front of your house. To amplify its appeal, choose colors that contrast well with the colors of your house. Yellows often work

English roses add a vertical element with their upright, bushy habit. Shown here is 'Symphony' (soft yellow).

beautifully with red or brown brick. Houses with light-colored exterior siding are flattered by rich reds, deep salmons and bright pinks. Pale pastels show up well when grown before a dark evergreen backdrop.

Two types of plant forms work well in foundation plantings: 1) bushy mounds such as 'Carefree Wonder' (pink), 'Margaret Merril' (lavender) and 'Sevillana' (red); and 2) leggy upright growers that are best described as semi-climbers. When given some support and pruned to control their height, semi-climbers become what are called pillars. Strategically placed pillars add vertical interest to foundation plantings along with much-needed color. Cultivars that may be handled this way include many of the David Austin English roses such as 'Heritage', and numerous Old Roses classified as Noisettes, Bourbons and Hybrid Musks.

The soft pinks of 'The Fairy' and other landscape roses make this house and stairway look inviting.

The purple of these petunias stands out when a light-brown mulch is used. Petunias can be hot companion plants, too.

SPECIMEN SHRUBS

'Rosa Mundi' (front) and 'Will Scarlet' are high-impact specimen plants.

TIP

ROSES WITH WATER

If your yard includes a small pond or other water feature, consider adding a specimen rose close to the water's edge. Since any water feature is a natural focal point, roses are premier plants to beautify the surrounding area. If your pond is framed in stone, use container-grown roses for this purpose. Light-colored blooms become even more noticeable when they reflect off the water's surface, and fallen petals floating in water are always delightful to behold.

A specimen shrub is just what the name implies—a plant that's so appealing that it is grown as a single spectacular specimen in a high-visibility spot. Many roses make excellent specimens, particularly multi-talented cultivars that seem to offer everything: lush foliage, beautiful fragrant flowers and the ability to bloom repeatedly when properly grown.

For any rose to perform well as a specimen shrub, it needs a very sunny, well-drained site that can be perfectly prepared to meet the needs of the plant. In some landscapes, this may mean creating an island bed that stands alone in a swath of lawn. Such a bed need not be circular in shape. Oblong or teardrop shaped beds in which an exuberant rose is the primary element are often more attractive than circles, squares or rectangles.

Specimens may also be added to large borders, or planted in sections of a foundation bed that extend out from the house, particularly at the front corners. Elongating a foundation planting so that it stretches out from the

GATEKEEPER ROSES

In small yards surrounded by a waist-high fence, the entry gate is a natural place for a specimen rose. Choose a rose that will grow 12 to 18 inches higher than the fence, in a color that coordinates well with the trim colors of your house. In this way, the rose will link the house and yard together. Some of the best roses for this use are vigorous Floribundas that produce large clusters of flowers for a big splash of color. Fine choices include coral 'Fashion' and pink 'Betty Prior'. With secure staking or a roomy arch for support, you can also use fragrant Hybrid Musks as specimen shrubs to grace any gateway. Some pruning will be needed to keep them within reasonable bounds.

Specimen beds containing many types of roses add to a home's appearance.

A closeup of 'Graham Thomas' shows why tough-growing, good-looking David Austin roses make great specimen plants in milder climates.

Soft pink 'Sparrieshoop' shows that a lighter-hued rose can make an excellent specimen.

TIP TIPS FOR REPEAT BLOOMERS

In general, it's best to approach the English roses as you might a vigorous Floribunda or climbing Hybrid Tea. Preserve non-blooming new canes that develop late in the summer, for they will produce flowers in late spring the following year. When those flowers are gone, prune the plants by up to one-third their size, allow them a brief rest, and then fertilize them to support a strong second flush of flowers in late summer. Especially in warm climates, it's not unusual for some English roses to work like Climbers in spring and Teas in late summer. In either form they make fine specimen shrubs, but remember that you have to reach all sides of the plants for maintenance purposes.

corner of a house emphasizes horizontal lines and makes the house appear wider. You can achieve a nice balance without making huge beds at both front corners of your house by developing one side into a bed that includes a large specimen rose, and anchoring the other side with a shapely ornamental tree.

Stellar Specimens

Roses used as specimen shrubs should have a full, bushy habit. In Zones 6 to 9 and protected places in Zone 5, many of the best roses to grow as specimen shrubs are the English roses bred by David Austin. Less angular than Hybrid Teas, these roses usually combine the tough constitution of Shrub roses with the fragrance and elegant blooms found in old Damask strains. Each is slightly different from the other, but all can be coaxed into reliable reblooming patterns when thoughtfully pruned and fertilized.

In colder climates, choose hardier roses that will become attractions when they are in bloom. Vigorous Hybrid Teas grafted onto hardy rootstocks often can survive Zone 3 winters with protection, but because of their angular form they are best planted in groups of three rather than as singular

specimens. Where you want a larger, bushier plant, consider cold-hardy Rugosa cultivars such as 'Blanc Double de Coubert' (white) or 'Hansa' (violet red). When the highly fragrant flowers fade, both of these selections produce a heavy crop of attractive hips.

Good Company

Companion plants for specimen shrubs can be quiet or rowdy, depending on the effect you want to achieve. Gray-foliage plants—lamb's ear, dusty miller and 'Silver Mound' artemisia—will add a luminous

Don't overlook Species roses, for example R. banksiae banksiae ("Lady Banks' Rose") when thinking about specimen roses.

glow to the specimen bed. Other low-key choices include purple ajuga, green pachysandra and variegated English ivy.

For riveting color, consider underplanting a specimen rose with spreading petunias such as 'Pink Wave'. Other excellent annuals for this purpose include portulaca (moss rose) and annual vincas.

Lamb's ear (Stachys byzantina 'Silver Carpet') and other silvery plants are good companions for specimen roses.

VERTICAL ACCENTS

Roses that reach for the sky are one of the few plants that can meld the garden's walls and ceiling with a visual flow. When grown vertically, long-limbed climbing roses naturally draw the eye upward, inviting us to enjoy not only the rose but the sky beyond.

Climbing roses, which we define here as any rose that habitually develops canes more than 10 feet long, can serve numerous landscaping purposes. We're accustomed to seeing climbing roses gingerly entwining themselves in metal arches, but many cultivars have so much growing energy that they will swallow such a structure within a few years' time. When landscaping with climbing roses, choose sites that make the most of the visual drama unique to these energetic plants. Climbing roses should never be required to whisper. Instead, encourage them to SHOUT!

Climbers require a little patience, for most need a year or two to establish themselves after being planted. During this juvenile period, give the plants excellent care in terms of water, fertilizer and pest control, and work along with their natural pattern of growth. With most climbers, it's best to choose a few long canes and train them vertically, and then switch to a more horizontal direction. This form helps the plants make use of available light and stimulates the growth of lateral branches (those that grow outward from the main canes). Lateral branches usually produce the most flowers.

Species Climbers like 'Paul's Scarlet Climber' need little training but require strong support.

When allowed to follow their natural growth pattern, very tall Climbers (often called "natural" Climbers) need little training after their first two or three years. They naturally grow into huge plants that cover arbors, pergolas or walls with thick foliage and a vigorous burst of flowers in early summer. Most natural climbers bloom heavily once a year, in early summer, and perhaps lightly a second time in late summer. Numerous Species roses and Old Roses

Basic Training

Climbing roses don't really climb, for they have no way of attaching themselves to support. This must be done by the gardener, either by tying the canes in place, by weaving the young green canes into a trellis, or by simultaneously weaving and tying the canes to a post, fence or other type of support.

'Zéphirine Drouhin' is a Bourbon that gives a refreshing lift as a climber.

*"Yellow Lady Banks' Rose" (*R. banksiae lutea*), here trained to an arbor, is a Species Rose that climbs and fills a vertical space.*

Daylilies can cover the spare lower growth of Climbers. Shown here is 'Charles Johnston'.

Upright accents welcome both the eye and the visitor.

classified as Noisettes and Bourbons are best handled as climbers or pillars, for they are naturally long-limbed plants.

With most natural climbers, any serious pruning is best done

PROMOTING GOOD "SPORTS-MANSHIP"

Climbing roses that are sports of Hybrid Teas and Floribundas, such as 'Climbing Peace' or 'Climbing Iceberg', are capable of blooming repeatedly when properly handled. However, since regular pruning is needed to help the plants push out new flowering buds, these roses seldom attain the height or size of natural climbers. Some English roses, although they aren't true sports, also show a strong tendency to climb in warm climates. When this happens, just let the plants have their way, and handle them just like climbing sports.

Prune climbing sports after the first flush of flowers fades by cutting back lateral branches to a bud just above a leaf that has 5 or 6 leaflets. Also top back extremely long canes that have overgrown their trellis. Prune plants again in early winter, taking only enough wood to make long canes more manageable and to remove stems that are obviously dead or diseased.

in summer after the flowering period ends. Cut out one or two of the old canes (which are dark brown or scaly gray) near the base of the plant so it will put more energy into the development of new flowering limbs. Inspect the plants every few weeks, and secure new canes as needed to keep them from whipping about in the wind. In early winter, clip back wayward stems and laterals as needed to restrain the plant, but remove as little growth as necessary. Leaf buds that emerge in spring will quickly be followed by flowers.

A Natural High with Climbers

- If your home has an attractive tile or wood shingle roof, you can call attention to it by training a vigorous Climber upward to the roofline, and then laterally around a window or entryway.
- In a small garden, use a climbing rose to structure the garden's wall while using a relatively small planting space.
- In a larger landscape where a strong shot of color is needed, the sinewy stems of Climbers can be trained to twist and tumble over a tall tripod made of cedar logs.
- Selected cultivars that grow to modest heights

can be used to dress upright posts. This form, called the pillar, works best with reblooming climbers that grow to less than 10 feet.
- When attaching climbers to exterior walls in espalier fashion, use the laterals to work the plants into living sculptures. Emphasizing the laterals results in heavier flowering.

Good Company

Healthy climbers are always top heavy, in that the lower portions of the plant appear bare compared with the lush foliage and flowers aloft. Broad-leafed foliage plants or ground-covers help to visually anchor climbing roses in place. Hostas are perfect for this job, or you can use clumps of liriope, ajuga or variegated sage.

'America' is an abundant, fragrant modern Climber.

'America', close-up.

ROSES FOR DECKS AND PATIOS

'Blue Mist' and other Miniatures are low-care, high-reward roses for planter boxes.

Growing roses on decks, patios, balconies or terraces is usually synonymous with growing them in containers.

Container culture offers several advantages over growing roses in the ground. If filled with the right soil mix, containers provide excellent drainage and you can closely control light exposure by moving your roses around. The primary challenge to growing containerized roses is the constant need to monitor moisture and fertilizer, but you can meet these needs easily if you're willing to spend a few relaxing minutes each day working with your plants.

Like other roses, those grown in containers require bright sun for most of the day. It's also important to note that containers placed in strong sun may heat up more than is comfortable for most roses. If you live in a hot climate, one smart strategy is to grow your roses in plastic pots (which retain moisture better than other types of containers), and slip the pots inside square wooden planters, which help keep the roses' roots shaded and cool. In cool summer climates where roses need all the heat they can get, grow them in dark-colored containers that help capture solar warmth.

Potted Beauties

Miniature roses will grow happily in containers only 12 inches wide, but bear in mind that small containers require more frequent watering than larger ones. If the site is roomy enough, you might want to grow three small Miniatures in a large rectangular planter rather than in individual pots. Small Floribundas, Hybrid Teas, and numerous thrifty Old Roses classified as Chinas also will grow quite well in containers, provided the pots are at least 16 inches deep.

Use a high-quality potting soil that drains well for container-grown roses. Before planting, mix a coated time-release fertil-

Miniatures—here, 'Woman's Day'—offer movable accents when grown in pots.

Minis thrive in hanging baskets too.

Patio planter boxes filled with roses bring everyday enjoyment to family living areas.

izer (e.g. Osmocote) into the potting soil, and make sure the medium is thoroughly dampened. Once established, feed your roses with a water-soluble fertilizer at least every two weeks. Alternatively, you can make a weak, but balanced, fertilizer solution in a watering can and use it each time you water your roses. Roses that show light green or yellow leaves and little new growth need more fertilizer. Plants that are dark green and vigorous, but produce only a few flowers, are probably being too well fed.

Frequent fertilization may cause the soil pH to become too acidic for roses, so it is wise to check the pH of soil in containers at least three times each year. This is easily done with an inexpensive pH test kit or an electronic pH monitor. If the pH dips below 6.0, correct it by mixing a tablespoon of lime with 2 cups of potting soil. Poke several holes into the soil with a pencil or slender screwdriver, then sprinkle the limed potting soil into the holes and over the soil's surface.

In many areas, salts and other contaminants in tap water make

Roses, like any other container plant, require the right soil mixture to thrive.

it necessary to repot container-grown roses annually. If you normally filter your drinking water, also filter the water you give to your roses.

In areas of extreme heat, you might investigate using the new time-release moisture medium ("AquaGuard" is one brand) that absorbs moisture and then releases it as the soil dries.

Patio Picks

Miniature roses fit easily in patio and deck gardens, and most are strong repeat bloomers when deadheaded regularly, as are Hybrid Teas. If fragrance is a priority, try red 'Starina' or lavender-pink 'Jennifer'. Many other Miniatures are outstanding for exhibition-quality blossoms, but not for fragrance.

Include a few larger plants in your container collection to give your garden height and fragrance. White 'Iceberg', peachy pink 'Fashion' and several other Floribundas are easily grown in containers. Selected Old Roses also make fine container specimens, especially lilac pink 'Hermosa' and several other Chinas. Fragrant antique roses that are nearly thornless, such as creamy white 'Marie Pavié', are particularly desirable.

So-called cascading Miniatures such as 'Red Cascade' and 'Magic Dragon' (both red) can be grown in large hanging baskets, provided you water and fertilize them

Colored containers can bring out the color accents of a rose and brighten any area.

regularly in hot weather. They also look outstanding when grown in whiskey barrels and trained to climb up a post or trellis. Handled this way, they are ideal vertical accents in any patio or deck garden.

Good Company

When petite cascading annuals such as sweet alyssum and lobelia are planted inside the rims of large containers, they help balance the upright forms of most roses. To infuse your container garden with color, fill a few pots with bright blue scaevola, or basket-of-gold alyssum, *(Aurinia* spp.). Petunias or cascading geraniums planted in hanging baskets are always a nice touch, as are plants with fragrant foliage such as scented geraniums, thymes and mints.

TIP · PORTABLE PLANTS

To make your roses easy to move, build or buy small wheeled pallets for the largest pots. This makes it easy to move roses to a highly visible position when they are at their peak, or to hide them from view when they are least attractive. During periods of very hot weather, you may find that your roses benefit from being shifted to a spot that offers partial shade. In winter, they'll need to be moved to a protected place, such as the base of a south-facing wall. Wheeled display platforms or pallets make moving the plants easy and convenient.

Sweet Alyssum 'Wonderland Mix'.

'Rise 'n' Shine' is a highly-rated Mini.

INVITING ENTRYWAYS

Simplicity is a great virtue when it comes to landscaping the entryway to your home. Think of the door itself as the focal point in this part of your landscape, and work backward in designing plantings that will make the entry more cheerful and inviting.

Regardless of the style of the rest of your landscape, entryway plantings that are symmetrical or strongly balanced usually work best. In a symmetrical scheme, two identical plants or plant groupings flank the landing or portion of the walkway closest to the door. A balanced design may use two different types of plants on either side of the entry, but they are nicely matched in terms of size and texture. With either approach, finding ways to make the entry attractive year-round is a primary challenge.

Above all, your entryway should be as open as possible, and wide enough so that two people can approach the door walking side by side. Roses that sprawl or develop long, cascading branches might create a safety hazard, so you need special roses for entryway plantings. Two types—tree roses and compact landscape roses—are the best choices to grow near walkways and doors.

Thornless 'Zéphirine Drouhin' is a people-friendly entryway rose that blooms over a long season and is fragrant.

Elegant Trees

Skilled nurserymen create tree roses, also called standard roses, by grafting Hybrid Tea or Floribunda roses onto the tops of tall rootstocks. The grafts form a tuft of blooming stems atop trunks 2 to 3 feet tall.

An entryway rose says "Welcome."

TIP

ACCENTING ENTRYWAY COLORS

To help highlight the roses in an entryway planting, enrich the scene with accents in contrasting colors. For example, if you use pink roses near the front door, put blue to work close by—by painting the door blue, using blue in chair cushions, or perhaps simply placing a blue mat by the front door. Use the same strategy with red roses, which are set off by pale yellow and white. If desired, add dark green as a third coordinating color.

Entryway roses encircle a doorway and create a natural vestibule.

Standardized roses, like this Floribunda 'Showbiz', are friendly guardians of entryways.

When placed on either side of an entryway, tree roses stand at attention as colorful sentinels. However, they are high-maintenance plants that require exacting care.

At all times, the trunk of a tree rose should be reinforced with a strong stake that reaches all the way up to the grafted head. During the summer, deadhead your tree roses every few days, and prune so that all sides of the top remain balanced. Except in Zones 8 and 9, tree roses need elaborate winter protection to keep the tops from being killed by stressful weather. You can dig them and move them to a cool but protected place in late fall, or partially dig them, lay them on their sides and mulch over the prostrate plants with sawdust and burlap.

There is, however, a much easier way to put the natural drama of tree roses to work in entryway plantings. Grow the roses in large nursery liners 14 inches across and 14 inches deep, and sink the planted pots into holes dug in the ground.

A row of 'Simplicity' lines a walk.

Place at least an inch of gravel or pebbles in the bottom of each hole for drainage. In fall when the roses stop blooming, move them to a cold garage or other protected location. In place of the roses, fill the "pot holes" with small upright evergreens, such as dwarf columnar junipers or arborvitae, planted in the same size containers as the roses. In this way, your entryway looks appealing through the winter, and your tree roses are subjected to much less trauma.

Delightful Drifts

Tree roses have a naturally formal shape, so they may look out of place in a very rustic landscape or cottage-type garden. To enrich informal entryways, consider planting small drifts of a compact landscape rose. A drift is a natural looking clump of at least three identical plants, set close enough so that they form a small mass. Excellent roses for this purpose include 'Carefree Wonder' (pink), 'Champlain' (red), or one of the new Flower Carpet series (pink to white). These cultivars bloom continuously and require only occasional trimming to keep them looking neat. They are also tremendously winter-hardy and need only a good mulch to help them survive cold winters.

When placing any roses near entryways, allow a 2-foot margin of space between the roses and where people walk. You can use this margin to add colorful annuals that will help frame the roses, or evergreens that provide winter interest. Or fill the margin with spring-flowering bulbs, such as tulips and daffodils, surrounded by an attractive mulch.

Good Company

Excellent edging annuals for entryway plantings include dwarf petunias, nierembergia, sweet alyssum and dusty miller. Since light-colored flowers are easily seen at night, they work almost like footlights along a front walkway. Good perennials for this purpose include evergreen candytuft, hardy geraniums, creeping thyme, ajuga and liriope. Choose small daffodils for planting along walkways. To help hide the fading bulb foliage, interplant bulbs with pansies or dwarf daylilies.

Ajugas are great groundcover perennials.

Candytuft (Iberis sempervirens) seems to glow at night.

MASS PLANTING

Rosa multiflora *used as a mass groundcover.*

If your property is large, you can use vigorous spreading roses to cover spacious areas that otherwise would require laborious mowing. When used this way, roses become an impenetrable year-round thicket covered with a colorful blanket of blooms in late spring and early summer. Areas covered with spreading roses also work well as wildlife habitats, for numerous birds and small animals such as chipmunks find food and shelter in a blooming briar patch.

Gentle slopes that are too rocky or awkward to mow also may be planted with spreading roses, provided you can find suitable planting areas on the slope. A few old Species Roses will grow in any sunny spot. For the most part, these tough antique strains bloom only once a year. Modern landscape roses that bloom repeatedly during the summer require better soil fertility if they are to produce more than one crop of flowers.

Mass rose plantings give you the opportunity to paint your landscape with color in broad strokes. If the site will be viewed from a distance, be sure to use some bright reds or deep pinks in your planting plan. These may be combined with selections that produce white, yellow or light pink flowers for riveting color contrast. When possible, plant the light colors behind the brighter ones to help accentuate the natural contrast between both the foliage and the flowers. Many spreading roses that produce bright blossoms also produce stems and leaves that are tinted with red.

Worrisome Weeds

Before planting roses in mass, do everything you can to rid the site of weeds. Most spreading roses will smother out small grassy weeds, but woody weeds—tree saplings, privet, and other invasive shrubs—have no trouble threading themselves upward through a tangle of rose canes. Don't worry about low, rambunctious winter weeds such as wild strawberries or creeping Charlie, which may form a thin groundcover beneath spreading roses. These will not interfere

A bare hillside becomes a smashing garden spectacle when covered with the right landscape rose—here, 'Bonica'.

with the growth of your roses, and may help prevent erosion from heavy winter rains.

Problems with woody weeds often recur a season or two after mass plantings have become established. For this reason, it is a good idea to carve strategic access lanes into a rose thicket so you'll have some way to reach into the planting to cut out woody weeds with long-handled loppers. Since spreading roses often multiply themselves by suckering (new plants grow from buds that form on shallow wandering roots) and by natural layering (low stems become covered with mulch or soil, and respond

This mass planting of roses and daylilies will cover this forest-edged hillside all summer long.

by developing roots), you will need to reopen your access lane at least every other winter, while the plants are dormant.

Feeding the Masses

Fertilize mass-planted roses every spring by broadcasting a time-release fertilizer over the root zones of the plants. All of the roses discussed below are so disease-resistant that they do not require spraying to control foliar diseases.

You may prune modest-sized mass plantings after they bloom to help encourage reblooming, but summer pruning of mass-planted roses is not required. Left unpruned, the thicket will perpetuate itself for several seasons. If the plants become so woody and overgrown that flowering becomes weak, you can rejuvenate a mass planting by mowing it 6 to 8 inches above the surface. This is best done with heavy equipment, such as the tractors and bush hog mowers used to clean roadside ditches.

Fast Spreaders

Where soil improvement is not practical, as on slopes or in rocky sites where planting pockets can be opened up between large stones, look to rambling Species roses for a groundcover effect. In areas where temperatures seldom drop below the mid-teens, "Lady Banks' Rose" (*R. banksiae*) is simply unbeatable. Fragrant, nearly thornless and absolutely rampant, it will cover a slope in a few seasons, or you can train the long canes up trees or over buildings. If you want a compara-

'Red Meidiland', like the rest of its family, is a quick spreader.

ble rose with thorns, consider 'Mermaid', a single yellow-flowered Rambler that has been smothering slopes and outbuildings for 80 years. In colder areas (to Zone 5), the pink-clustered roses often seen growing on country roadsides are great for mass planting or growing into a groundcover. Their lineage can be linked to the species rose known as *R. multiflora carnea*, often called "Seven Sisters."

Numerous spreading roses with "Meidiland" in their name are excellent candidates for mass planting in Zones 4 to 9. Meidiland cultivars are available in a wide range of colors and both single and double flowers. In addition to the Meidilands, consider other hardy spreading roses such as 'Carefree Delight' and 'Sea Foam', both of which are pink.

Good Company

In mass plantings that need a backdrop, install a second mass planting of large ornamental grasses. Besides providing a visual frame, *Miscanthus*, *Pennisetum* and other species that grow into thick clumps work as an effective barrier to stop the spread of roses to areas where they are not wanted. Use hardy naturalized bulbs such as daffodils or narcissus as foreground plants.

CRAFTER'S CORNER

Miniature 'Minnie Pearl' (pink blend), Shrub 'Abraham Darby' (orange-pink), Shrub 'Graham Thomas' (yellow), Shrub 'Mary Rose' (medium pink), and phlox 'Mt. Fuji' are a bouquet ready to happen.

The pleasure of growing roses does not have to end when the last petals fall to the ground. If you enjoy crafts, you'll certainly like preserving buds and blossoms to use in dried bouquets and sachets.

All types of roses can be dried for potpourri, but expanding your rose collection to include special, historically important types will enrich and authenticate every project you undertake. Of particular interest are Gallicas, Damasks and Bourbons, for these roses produce distinctive fragrances that often persist after the blossoms have dried. (Chapter 3 provides historical background information on these venerable old strains of roses.)

In the modern landscape, each type of rose needs a special environmental niche based on its size and form. The planting site will also influence the plants' health; for example, Bourbons are quite susceptible to black spot and need good air circulation. Locate highly fragrant roses in different parts of your garden so you can discern each one's distinctive fragrance.

When incorporating these or other "keeping" roses into your landscape, also bear in mind that like most Old Roses, these cultivars normally bloom heavily only once every year. Although the exact bloom time varies from region to region, Old Roses typically bloom in late spring and early summer. Most of the blossoms develop from healthy canes that grew the year before, so any pruning done in spring must be very light.

Gallica roses that date back to medieval France are the medicinal roses of the past. The plants themselves are sturdy bushes 3 to 5 feet tall and equally wide. Thorns are few and far between, so Gallicas are good roses to place near traffic areas where more prickly plants will not do. Pink is the most common color, as reflected in the strain known as 'Apothecary's Rose', but there are also reds such as 'Charles de Mills'. A single mature Gallica can scent an entire garden, especially during the morning hours.

Gallica roses usually bloom promptly after new growth emerges in spring. Allow the blossoms to open fully before gathering them, and let some of the blossoms ripen naturally so you can go back and harvest the hips in late fall.

Many old **Damask Roses** can be traced to the dry climate of the Middle East. These are arching plants that require plenty of room, and may be difficult to fit into a small garden. All shades of pink can be found in the fragrant Damasks. Damask Roses, including pink 'Kazanlik' and the wonderful creamy-white 'Mme. Hardy', bloom heavily in early summer, and occasionally later in the season as well.

'Belle Portugaise' petals ready to dry.

Damasks work well when grown as single specimens in an open lawn, or you can place one at the end of a border and let its cascading stems become fragrant fountains of color. Most Damasks coordinate perfectly with forsythias, which are arching shrubs that bloom very early in spring. For a fragrant and colorful boundary grouping, try growing a single Damask between and slightly in front of two forsythias.

Bourbon roses provide an opportunity to enjoy the fragrance and beauty of Damasks in a smaller space. They do, however, require excellent light exposure and air circulation to prevent problems with black spot. To be on the safe side, place Bourbons at least 15 feet away from other more susceptible roses to avoid movement of spores in wind-blown rain. Since the canes of Bourbons are both arching and stiff, they are perfect plants to peg into mounds. 'Mme. Isaac Pereire' and several other cultivars are excellent candidates for this treatment, described at right.

Good Company

Since most Old Roses look their worst in late summer, station fall-blooming sedum 'Autumn Joy', chrysanthemums or asters nearby to bring color to the garden. Narrow-leaf zinnias work well as foreground plants all summer long.

Ornamental grasses combine well with roses and offer craft opportunities.

PEGGING A BOURBON

Plant the rose on a low mound that has a slight slope, and allow it to grow freely for a year. Keep the area beneath the rose free of weeds and heavily mulched. In the second spring, when leaves are beginning to emerge, select 5- to 6-foot-long canes for pegging. Gently scrape away the leaves attached to each section of cane within six inches of the tip, preserving the growing tip. Use hoops made of 10-gauge wire to secure the bare sections of cane to the ground, so that the cane arches over gracefully at least 8 inches above the soil. Remove the wire hoops when the flowering period ends, and trim canes to help them rise higher above the ground.

Drying a heady mix of roses.

BOUNTEOUS BORDERS

A border is a special type of flower bed which is a great favorite of people who just like to grow flowers. English gardeners developed the border concept, which includes several distinct features. A proper border always has a backdrop, which can be trees, a fence or a grouping of tall shrubs. Within the border, the tallest plants are placed in the rear, so that each can be easily seen. At least 4 feet of depth is needed to accommodate three or more layers of plants. Most borders are at least 20 feet long.

Since roses come in so many different shapes and sizes, you can use them in endless ways in a border-type bed. Tall upright Rugosas work well in the back of a border, where their fall foliage colors and early winter hips help extend the season. Softly contoured English roses and Old Roses trained to a pillar form make ideal vertical elements for the middle of the border, and you can put little Miniatures to work along the border's front edge.

However, you don't always have to arrange plants in order of height within your border. Occasionally, bringing a tall plant forward helps to keep the border interesting, and it may benefit the plant as well. An excellent example might be a Hybrid Tea rose such as rich red 'Mister Lincoln'. As do other Hybrid Teas, 'Mister Lincoln' needs excellent air circulation to

TIP

SOLID SEMI-CLIMBERS

The back of the border is a great place for 6-foot-tall pillar roses, which may be old Bourbons, Noisettes, or leggy English Roses. Train them to hug a stout wood post or an iron trellis. Make sure you include a pathway or series of steppingstones that lead toward the pillar to make it easy to collect fragrant blossoms and attend to regular maintenance chores.

prevent disease problems, and its blossoms are so pretty and fragrant that the plant deserves to be placed where you can easily touch and smell the blossoms. Try placing 'Mister Lincoln' toward the front of a border, amid high-contrast companion plants such as white Shasta daisies or pale blue pansies.

Weaving Roses into the Border

In a classic English border, the majority of the plants are perennials. You can certainly emphasize perennials in your border, but few regions in North America have weather as kind to perennials as the cool maritime climate of England. Instead, go ahead and accent roses in your border if you like, for borders often work best when one type of plant is prominently represented so that there is a lot of one thing (like roses). Then use annuals, bulbs and carefully selected perennials as companion plants.

Miniatures 'Orange Honey' and 'Rise 'n' Shine' anchor this sunny border.

Hybrid Teas aren't just for cutting gardens. Here, 'Mister Lincoln' thrives in a mixed border with viola, lady's mantle, foxglove and sedum.

Look beyond flower color when choosing plants to grow alongside roses in the border. Foliage texture and color are tremendously important, because foliage remains while flowers come and go. It is also critical that companion plants not crowd or block the light and air that roses need to stay healthy. At the same time, you do not want to have a border filled with large empty pockets. Small annuals such as pansies, petunias and vincas can help fill all of these needs.

Plan Ahead for Seasonal Change

To help your border look attractive throughout the year, incorporate plants that bloom at different times. Identify the bloom times of your roses, and then add plants that bloom at other times. Spring-blooming bulbs announce the new growing year, and you can use summer-blooming daylilies to help hide the fading foliage from daffodils and tulips. For fall color, make a late sowing of marigolds, set out potted chrysanthe-

Coreopsis 'Moonbeam' and blue fescue form a border with rose 'Pink Meidiland'.

mums, and give some thought to showy native goldenrods and asters. Most reblooming roses put on a great show in the fall, too.

Good Company

When growing bushy English roses in a border, consider underplanting them with perennial wildflowers that prefer the shade. Soft pink or blue hardy geraniums (known as cranesbills) work very well, as do pale blue Drummond phlox and yellow Celandine poppies. These woodland wildflowers usually bloom early in spring, several weeks ahead of roses. In summer, use yellow 'Moonbeam' coreopsis or "Yellow Gem" marigolds to hide the bare ankles of angular Hybrid Teas.

'New Dawn' works in a border and as a Climber too.

THE SECRET OF A SUCCESSFUL BORDER

The versatility that makes borders so much fun comes with a price that must be paid up front, when the bed is first created. You should provide excellent drainage, cultivate to at least 18 inches, and make sure the soil has the texture of potting soil. If your soil is very porous sand or extremely heavy clay, consider excavating the soil and filling the bed with humus-rich topsoil before you start planting a border. Short of excavation, amend the soil with copious amounts of rotted manure, compost and other rich types of organic matter.

GALLERY OF COMPANION PLANTS

Rugosa roses make effective borders and hedges.

Ten Easy Annuals

Alyssum
(*Lobularia maritima*)
Sweet alyssum is a cool-season annual that spreads into a soft carpet of white, lavender or purple. Set out plants in spring. Space plants only 4 inches apart if you want them to grow together into a nice edging. This little annual is extremely useful in containers and window boxes, or for planting among steppingstones. Many selections are lightly fragrant.

Dusty miller
(*Senecio cineraria*)
A soft gray foliage plant, dusty miller is a versatile annual that goes with everything. Set out bedding plants in spring, and pinch back tops to encourage bushy growth, or they will get leggy. Dusty miller goes especially well with pink or red roses. It is often winter-

hardy in Zones 7 to 9, but usually looks best when handled as a summer annual.

Gypsophila
(*Gypsophila elegans*)
Commonly called baby's breath, annual gypsophila grows into soft cloudlike mounds covered with tiny mauve-pink blossoms. Closely spaced plants make a great edging, or you can plant them in drifts among tall roses. Set out bedding plants in spring, and mulch to prevent problems with annual weeds. Perennial baby's breath (*G. paniculata*) is much larger, and best grown in a roomy bed or border.

Marigold
(*Tagetes* hybrids)
All marigolds are warm-weather annuals available in a range of sizes and colors. Sow seeds or set out bedding plants in spring. For fall color, sow a second crop

of seedlings in midsummer. Stick with soft yellow marigolds for planting near red, coral, or deep pink roses, and choose dwarf varieties with numerous small blossoms. Gem or signet marigolds produce lush fragrant foliage and tiny single flowers.

Pansy
(*Viola* x *wittrockiana*)
Cold-hardy pansies can be planted in fall in Zones 4 to 9, but they may get ragged in rough winter weather. You can also plant them first thing in spring. Start with bedding plants to save time. The compact plants flower continuously until hot weather arrives in summer. The color range is extensive, but white, blue, and yellow work best with roses. Use pansies as edging plants, or plant them among daffodils, tulips, and other spring-flowering bulbs.

Petunia (*Petunia* hybrids)
Petunias bring a special softness to the garden, which contrasts beautifully with the texture of roses. Choose heavy-blooming white or pink floribunda types for edging beds. Spreading petunias such as 'Pink Wave' or 'Purple Wave' grow into colorful summer groundcovers when planted beneath Hybrid Teas. Set out bedding plants in spring. In mid-

summer, trim plants back by half to promote strong reblooming in the fall.

Portulaca
(*Portulaca* hybrids)
Also called Moss Rose, portulaca thrives in hot weather and full sun. The blooms resemble Miniature roses. Set out bedding plants in late spring, or sow the tiny seeds beneath widely spaced roses. Portulaca is ideal for edging beds or planting among steppingstones, and also makes a good summer filler for borders in warm climates. Mixtures usually include plants that flower in yellow, white, pink, orange and rose red.

Scaevola
(*Scaevola aemula*)
Also known as blue fan flower, scaevola is a dependable source of the blue color that's so scarce during the warm summer season. Grow

Rose hips on Rugosas can be as large as cherry tomatoes.

'Simplicity' acts as a colorful foundation planting.

purchased plants in containers, or plant them in borders in warm climates. Scaevola is a must-have for container or patio gardens, because it's a nonstop summer bloomer. Display it near any color or type of rose, especially red, orange or yellow roses.

Snapdragon
(*Antirrhinum majus*)

You can set out bedding plants of snapdragons first thing in spring. When new growth develops, pinch back the main stem to encourage bushiness. Choose dwarf varieties for planting near roses. Soft yellow, pink or white blend well with most rose hues. Naturally upright and formal, snapdragons also make long-lasting cut flowers.

Zinnia
(*Zinnia angustifolia*)

Narrowleaf zinnias are different from other garden zinnias. They bloom tirelessly for months, producing hundreds of starry single blossoms, and are highly resistant to powdery mildew. Set out bedding plants in spring, and pinch off the tops to encourage bushy growth. Orange selections are widely available, but white ones usually work better with roses.

Four Great groundcovers

Ajuga
(*Ajuga reptans*)

Hardy to Zone 3, ajuga develops rosettes of purple, green or variegated foliage that spread into a thick mass. Also known as carpet bugleweed, this groundcover produces bright blue flower spikes in late spring. Use ajuga as an edging plant around rose beds, or plant it along walkways. Dig and replant every few years to keep ajuga from becoming so overgrown that it does not flower well.

English Ivy
(*Hedera helix*)

This beautiful vine is well worth the discipline required to keep it from spreading where it's not wanted. Hardy to Zone 5, English ivy can be used as an edging or groundcover, or for growing on a wall near climbing roses. Variegated varieties require more shade than green-leafed ones, which grow best in partial sun. Set out new plants in spring, and be prepared to wait a year before seeing vigorous growth.

Liriope
(*Liriope muscari; L. spicata*)

Often called monkey grass or lilyturf, liriope is best used as a green edging plant in Zones 4 to 10. Set out plants in spring or early fall, and plant them in broad bands for maximum visual effect. Variegated types tolerate substantial sun, and usually grow into circular clumps that require dividing every 3 or 4 years. Trim back brown foliage in late winter to make way for fresh new leaves.

Pachysandra
(*Pachysandra terminalis*)

Evergreen in Zones 5 to 9, pachysandra is a fine groundcover for growing beneath hedge roses because it naturally smothers out weeds. This plant does require rich soil and regular water, or it will not perform well. Set out new plants in spring. Fertilize annually when new growth begins by digging in some good compost or

Asiatic lilies look good with Shrub roses.

rotted manure. Variegated forms make beautiful accents for the edges of beds.

Ten Prime Perennials

Artemisia
(*Artemisia* spp.)

This large plant family includes numerous woody shrubs with soft gray foliage that provides good color contrast for roses. Grow in good sun, and trim plants regularly to encourage bushy growth. Use the cuttings in flower arrangements. Avoid invasive species by planting only named cultivars, such as 'Powis Castle' (Zones 6 to 9), 'Silver Mound' (Zones 5 to 8), and 'Valerie Finnis' (Zones 4 to 8).

Hardy geraniums are wonderful underplanting choices to cover the bare lower stems of roses.

Delphiniums and scabiosa help accent the Hybrid Tea 'Chablis'.

Nicotiana (flowering tobacco) is a sweet-scented companion of 'Mary Rose'.

Candytuft
(*Iberis sempervirens*)

Grow this little evergreen plant wherever you want a puffy mound of white flowers in late spring. Hardy to Zone 3, candytuft works very well when spilling over the edges of beds framed with brick, stone or landscaping timbers. Cut back the plants after the flowers fade, and weed regularly for the remainder of the season. New plantings may be made, or old ones divided, in early fall or first thing in spring. A

few selections rebloom in late autumn.

Coreopsis
(*Coreopsis verticillata*)

Of the many species of coreopsis, the best for growing among roses are the 'Moonbeam' and 'Zagreb' cultivars. Single yellow flowers dance atop soft, finely cut green foliage through most of the summer. Plant them in

small clumps or drifts in front of bright red roses, or use them to draw attention to pale pink ones. Plants are easily divided in either fall or spring. They flower best when grown in sunny sites with fleeting shade from nearby roses.

Daffodil
(*Narcissus* spp.)

Of all the pretty bulbs that bloom in spring, none are more dependable or long-lived than durable daffodils. They naturalize in sites that get winter sun and summer shade. Use them to accent walkways and entries. Small daffodils can be planted beneath any type of rose, and work especially well with large shrubby types. To assure strong reblooming, always allow daffodil foliage to remain in the garden until it dies back naturally in early summer.

Daylily
(*Hemerocallis* hybrids)

Low-maintenance perennials, daylilies may be grown as single specimens or in much larger masses. They are great for combining with daffodils, for the new foliage of the daylilies hides the fading leaves of its companion. Dwarf reblooming daylilies such as 'Stella D'Oro' are ideal for framing the outer edges of rose beds, or for intermittent planting along walkways. Divide them every few years in either spring or fall.

Dianthus
(*Dianthus* spp.)

Numerous dianthus make fine additions to any garden, but spreading groundcover types such as grassy gray-green 'Bath's Pink' work especially well with roses. Provided drainage

'Charles Austin' in a mixed border.

'Dorothy Perkins' entwined with honeysuckle, Lonicera japonica 'Halliana'.

Lamb's ears and petunias accompany a mass planting of standardized 'The Fairy'.

Foxglove *with 'Mary Rose'.*

White roses contrast well with purples and blues.

'American Pillar' combined with Clematis jackmanii.

is excellent, this fragrant pink bloomer will grow into a cascading edging plant that retains its stiff foliage year-round. Hardy to Zone 4, this type of dianthus is best divided at least every two years, preferably in early summer after the flowers fade.

Geranium
(*Geranium* spp.)

Unlike the summer annuals or pot plants (*Pelargoniums*) known as geraniums, perennial geraniums (often called cranesbill) will persist in the garden year after year. In spring, they produce soft pink or lilac blossoms atop soft green foliage. Perennial geraniums grow well under roses, and benefit from the shade of tall English Roses and other

bushy cultivars. Hardy to Zone 4, these domesticated wildflowers usually spread slowly and re-seed themselves in hospitable sites.

Sage, Blue
(*Salvia superba*)

This 2-foot-tall, fountain-shaped perennial with gray foliage shines like a beacon when planted behind small bushy roses. In mid- to late summer, the tall stems are studded with vibrant blue flowers, which make welcome additions to cut arrangements. Long-lived, easy to grow, and hardy to Zone 5, blue sage is easily propagated by rooting stem cuttings taken in spring. Other perennial sage species include low, mounding selections with fragrant variegated leaves.

Stachys
(*Stachys byzantina* or *lanata*)

Commonly known as lamb's ear, this perennial can be

grown as a clump-forming plant or a groundcover. The gray leaves are so soft that they seem to be covered with downy fur. Hardy to Zone 4, stachys illuminates shady corners where roses cast their shadows during part of the day. To keep this plant looking its best, take up and replant small rooted rosettes in either spring or fall.

Thyme
(*Thymus* spp.)

Most thymes are naturally sprawling plants, which makes them easy to use as small groundcovers or

edging plants. The best tasting culinary thymes have green leaves; other selections with variegated silver or gold leaves are more ornamental when grown beneath roses. All produce little pink flowers in spring, which gives the plants a foamy appearance. The hardiest strains withstand winters to Zone 4, or you can dig them in the fall and keep them indoors in containers through winter.

Clematis jackmanii *growing into the Floribunda 'Westerland'.*

Herbs, including lavender (shown here) and thyme, can be sweet accents to roses.

'Orange Honey', like so many Miniatures, transforms the way we think about landscape plants.

◆ CHAPTER 5 ◆

TECHNIQUES

Roses have an undeserved reputation for being prima donnas. You know, beautiful, even brilliant—but so touchy and hard to get along with. Well, that's a bum rap! You can grow vigorous, healthy, *cooperative* plants by selecting the right rose based on your climate and your use, and then providing it with its basic cultural requirements.

As we've discussed in previous chapters, roses have diverse parentage, originating in different parts of the world with very different growing conditions. As a result there truly is a rose—and usually several different roses—that will grow well in almost any garden situation.

Gardening with Foresight

The first step in planning a successful rose planting is to be familiar with your general climatic conditions. The second step is to understand your particular site and growing conditions. There are many factors that influence the vigor of roses:

- winter hardiness
- summer heat extremes
- exposure
- precipitation
- soil moisture
- soil type and nutrition
- humidity
- snow cover
- cultural factors
- the general health of the rose when you purchase it

By understanding these factors, selecting rose classes and varieties that are well adapted to your growing conditions, and providing the appropriate cultural care, you can easily grow beautiful roses that don't require excessive maintenance.

As you read through this chapter, keep in mind the old saying, "right plant, right place, right way."

CLIMATES AND MICROCLIMATES

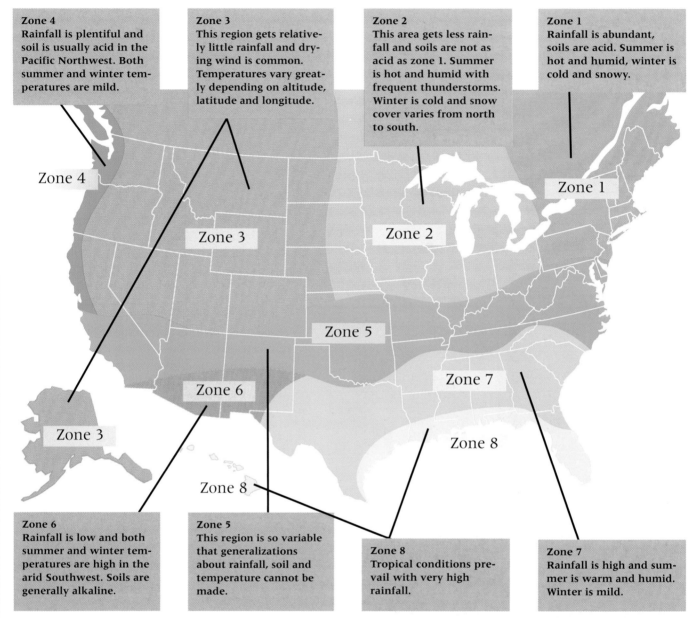

Zone 4
Rainfall is plentiful and soil is usually acid in the Pacific Northwest. Both summer and winter temperatures are mild.

Zone 3
This region gets relatively little rainfall and drying wind is common. Temperatures vary greatly depending on altitude, latitude and longitude.

Zone 2
This area gets less rainfall and soils are not as acid as zone 1. Summer is hot and humid with frequent thunderstorms. Winter is cold and snow cover varies from north to south.

Zone 1
Rainfall is abundant, soils are acid. Summer is hot and humid, winter is cold and snowy.

Zone 4

Zone 1

Zone 3

Zone 2

Zone 3

Zone 5

Zone 7

Zone 6

Zone 8

Zone 8

Zone 6
Rainfall is low and both summer and winter temperatures are high in the arid Southwest. Soils are generally alkaline.

Zone 5
This region is so variable that generalizations about rainfall, soil and temperature cannot be made.

Zone 8
Tropical conditions prevail with very high rainfall.

Zone 7
Rainfall is high and summer is warm and humid. Winter is mild.

The United States and Canada have eight general climate types, not to be confused with Hardiness Zones.

We live in a country with great geographic and climatic diversity. Because of variation in geography and climate across the United States, different regions display a wide variety of plants and gardening styles. A xeriscape (drought-tolerant) garden in New Mexico is decidedly different in style and plant species from a cottage garden in Massachusetts. Although hundreds of garden and plant variations occur, most gardeners in this country can grow at least one class of rose, and usually several classes, that will stand up to almost any existing climatic challenge.

In order to make the best choice of roses for your garden, it is crucial to match the appropriate rose classes with the climate in which you garden, the weather challenges you face and the microclimates on your property.

Climate

Climate is the collective state of the earth's atmosphere at a specific place over a long period of time. Climate is made up of such measurable factors as annual precipitation, tempera-

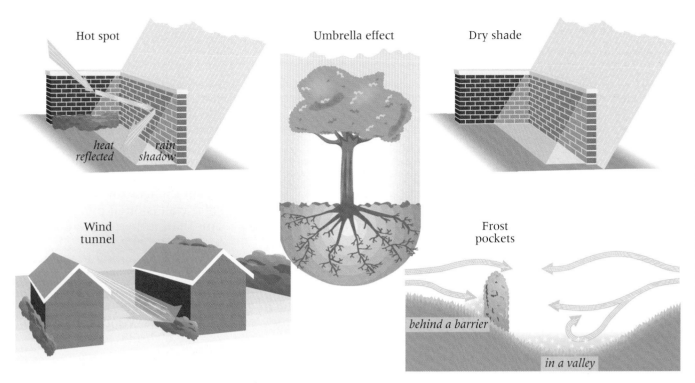

Hot spot

heat reflected *rain shadow*

Umbrella effect

Dry shade

Wind tunnel

Frost pockets

behind a barrier

in a valley

Microclimates can seriously affect how your roses grow.

ture highs and lows, and the number of frost-free days.

There is little you can do to change climate. Instead, it is best to become familiar with the kinds of roses that thrive in your climate and give them the cultural care they prefer.

There are several resources you can tap for detailed information about your specific climate, including your county extension service, Master Gardener organizations and hotlines and the U.S. Department of Agriculture (USDA).

Microclimates

In addition to regional climatic differences, nearly every garden has pockets that have specialized growing conditions. *Microclimate* is the term given to the sum of these various local factors including exposure, shade, moisture, wind and slope. Microclimates vary greatly within USDA Hardiness Zones, within cities and towns, and even within individual gar-

dens. Take advantage of microclimates in your garden to plant rose varieties that need the special growing conditions a microclimate provides.

Exposure

The most common microclimate conditions are created by exposure—the direction your garden faces. Exposure affects soil and air temperature, soil moisture and the amount of sunlight a planting site receives.

Some garden sites do not face a particular direction so they get sunlight equally from all southern directions all day long. This is referred to as full exposure.

North-facing gardens or slopes (and to a lesser extent, east-facing sites) warm more slowly in the spring, stay cooler throughout the growing season and retain more soil moisture. Also, plants come into bloom later here. Reserve these sites for later blooming, more cold-tolerant roses.

South- and west-facing planting sites are just the opposite. Select roses that thrive in

warmer summer temperatures and drier soil.

If your garden exposure is related to a physical structure, that is, located on the side of your house, barn or another building, then the amount and intensity of sunlight becomes a factor.

A garden (or at least part of it) on the north side of a building is in deep shade most of the day. This is not a good location for sun-loving roses! An east-side garden generally receives morning light and afternoon shade. If you live in Colorado where sunlight is intense, summer moisture is sparse and the air is dry, this might be a good place to grow pastel-colored roses. Pastel colors fade quickly in bright sun and dry conditions. A south-side garden generally receives full sun all day and a west-side garden is usually shaded in the morning and blasted by sun after noon.

A light-colored, west-facing wall creates wide temperature extremes that make a stressful growing environment. This site is in cool shade during the morning hours. Then, when the sun peaks over the structure, a light-colored wall reflects heat and light, causing air temperature to leap suddenly. Hot spots also occur in corners of walls, where air is usually still.

Moisture

The amount of natural moisture your roses receive depends on a number of factors. Natural moisture comes in the form of rain, snow and ground water. Rain and snow can be blocked by structures, creating areas that receive little or no rainfall.

Moisture and shade are often related. Areas of dry shade exist near walls and around large trees. The leeward side of a wall remains dry, as does the area under an overhang. If plants are placed in these microclimates, considerable supplemental water may be required.

Dry shade also exists above tree roots. Tree roots usually stretch beyond the outermost spread of the tree's branches, and absorb great amounts of moisture. Moist shade occurs at the bottom of a shaded slope and is better suited to astilbe than roses.

The kind of soil in your garden can also create a moisture microclimate. You might have fast-draining loam in some areas and water-logged, clay backfill in other areas. You can improve your soil conditions by adding amendments, but first you must be aware of the soil variations on your property to take the proper corrective steps. (See pp. 94–95 for information on soil preparation.)

Wind

If you live near the seashore, or in western Kansas, in Illinois or a host of other places buffeted by high winds, you know how devastating they can be to plants. In addition to the physical beating plants take from strong winds, they also suffer from moisture loss. Sustained wind causes soil to dry out, which robs plant roots of moisture. Even if the soil stays moist, plants often cannot remove moisture fast enough to keep up with increased transpiration losses due to wind. The plant finally shuts down, and wind burn and scorching occur.

If you garden in fear of that grisly scene, don't give up hope! There are several steps you can take to prevent wind burn.

1) Select an appropriate rose for a windy site. For example, Rugosa Roses are renowned for their performance in seashore gardens where wind is constant.

2) Provide a windbreak in the form of a fence or a screen of shrubs. The ideal windbreak has about two-thirds solid matter and one-third small holes. This breaks up large gusts and allows air to move through in smaller chunks. A windbreak of this sort cuts the wind significantly for a distance of twice the height of the windbreak. It does some good up to 10 times the height of the barrier. You definitely don't want to use a solid wall as a windbreak—the air on the leeward side of a solid wall is often more turbulent than if there were no break there at all.

3) Avoid planting in wind tunnels, which are created when wind is forced through narrow passages between buildings or trees. Wind tunnels will act like a cosmic hair dryer on your plants!

Slope

Growing conditions vary greatly from the top of a hill to the bottom. Hilltops are windier and drier than low areas. Cold air moves like water, running downhill until it reaches a barrier. Then it spreads out, up and over (depending on the height of the barrier). If there is no barrier, the air simply settles in low spots and creates a frost pocket.

If you decide to put roses in a low area, select varieties that are hardy to at least one zone cooler than your zone. For instance, if you live in USDA Plant Hardiness Zone 6, select rose varieties hardy to Zone 5 for planting in low areas.

WESTERN CLIMATES: A WILD AND WOOLLY MIX

The Western United States—the area between the Pacific Ocean and the Rocky Mountains—is a region with mild winters at lower elevations, long cold winters at upper elevations and limited water supplies all around. These factors make western gardening a world unto its own with unique horticultural laws.

Western climate zones are so diverse that they have been classified into 24 different climatic zones based on latitude, elevation, influence of the Pacific Ocean, influence of the continental air mass, mountains and hills, and local terrain.

The best advice? Carefully consider each of the microclimate factors outlined here.

HARDINESS AND HEAT

USDA Plant Hardiness Zone Map

One way to determine if a particular rose will grow in your garden is to know both the United States Department of Agriculture (USDA) Plant Hardiness Zone in which you garden, and the USDA Hardiness Zone rating of the rose. These well-established systems are generally the first thing to consider when selecting roses for your garden.

The USDA Plant Hardiness Zone Map uses the average annual minimum temperature to assign plant hardiness zone ratings to the United States, Canada and Mexico.

Correspondingly, plants are assigned a hardiness zone rating based on the lowest temperature they will survive. (Catalogs and labels carry those hardiness ratings.) For example, it wouldn't be wise to try to grow white Flower Carpet roses—Zone 6 plants that withstand an average minimum temperature of 0° to -10°F—in Zone 4 northern Iowa, where the average minimum temperature is -20° to -30°F. A better choice would be a rose like 'Charles Albanel' from the extremely cold-tolerant "Explorer" series. It has a similar growth habit but is hardy to Zone 3 (-30° to -40°F).

Plant Heat-Zone Map

Selecting roses based on their adaptability to summer heat is just as important as selecting roses based on their ability to withstand winter cold. While extreme cold temperature will almost immediately kill a rose that is not hardy, prolonged heat usually has the effect of causing

The USDA Plant Hardiness Zone Map indicates areas ("Zones") with similar average low temperatures. Use this in conjunction with a rose's hardiness rating (found in catalogs and on plant labels) to select roses that will tolerate your area's coldest temperatures.

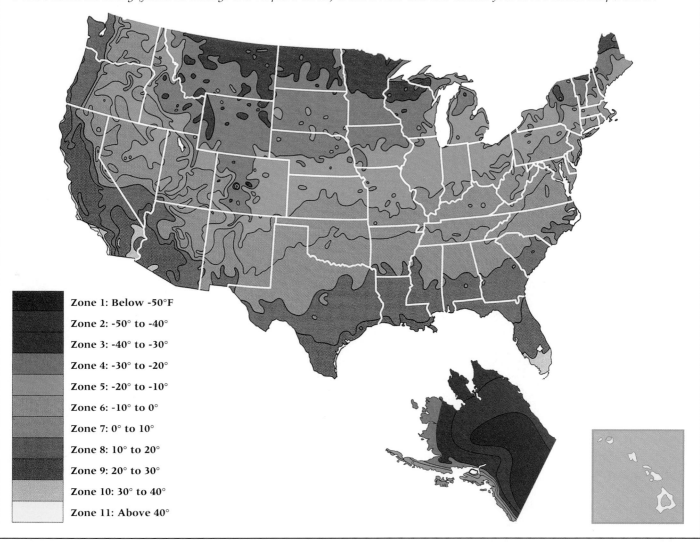

Zone 1: Below -50°F
Zone 2: -50° to -40°
Zone 3: -40° to -30°
Zone 4: -30° to -20°
Zone 5: -20° to -10°
Zone 6: -10° to 0°
Zone 7: 0° to 10°
Zone 8: 10° to 20°
Zone 9: 20° to 30°
Zone 10: 30° to 40°
Zone 11: Above 40°

an ill-suited rose to languish over several years and die a slow, painful death. By selecting roses that are adapted to your summer temperatures, you will have larger blooms with more intense colors—as well as a plant that flourishes year after year.

Leaves often show heat damage by wilting or turning brown. Recurrent-blooming roses may produce fewer, smaller blooms when heat-stressed. Roses suffering from heat damage do not die immediately. Instead, plants languish, looking chlorotic or stunted for several years before finally dying.

To help determine a plant's adaptability to heat, the American Horticultural Society (AHS) published the Plant Heat-Zone Map, which divides the United States into 12 zones, according to the number of days when temperatures typically rise above 86°F. (This is the temperature at which many plants suffer heat damage.) Heat damage is most severe when the air temperature is high for several consecutive days and, at the same time, soil moisture is in short supply.

As more and more roses are rated for heat tolerance it will be easier to select the appropriate rose for your heat zone.

Humidity

Relative humidity is a measure of the amount of water in the air compared with the amount of water the air can hold at any given temperature. Areas of the country like the Southeast and the central Midwest are much higher in humidity than the continental West.

Roses descended from tropical areas of the world, like Tea roses, grow much better in areas with high heat and humidity than do Rugosa roses, which generally prefer drier air.

Black spot, the most common rose disease in the United States (except in the arid West and

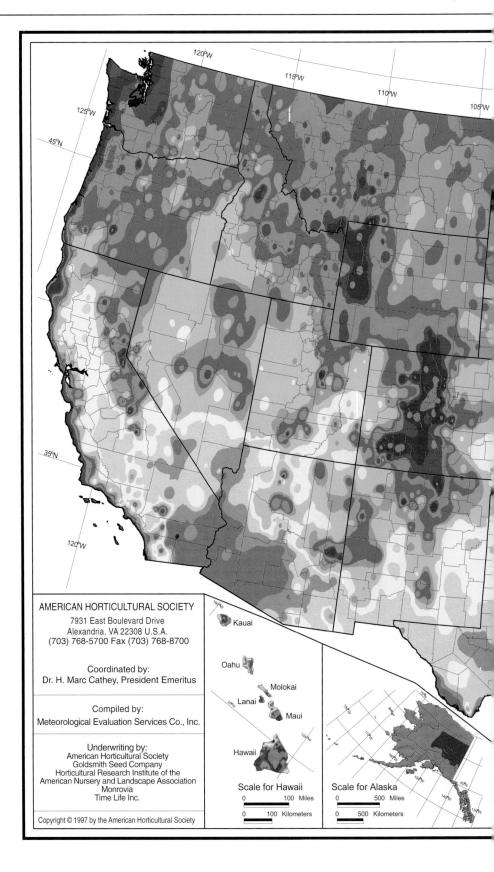

AMERICAN HORTICULTURAL SOCIETY

7931 East Boulevard Drive
Alexandria, VA 22308 U.S.A.
(703) 768-5700 Fax (703) 768-8700

Coordinated by:
Dr. H. Marc Cathey, President Emeritus

Compiled by:
Meteorological Evaluation Services Co., Inc.

Underwriting by:
American Horticultural Society
Goldsmith Seed Company
Horticultural Research Institute of the
American Nursery and Landscape Association
Monrovia
Time Life Inc.

Copyright © 1997 by the American Horticultural Society

Scale for Hawaii
0   100 Miles
0   100 Kilometers

Scale for Alaska
0   500 Miles
0   500 Kilometers

Southwest), thrives in hot, humid climates. The easiest way to avoid this devastating fungal disease is to plant varieties that are strongly black spot resistant. Another way is to plant where there is good air circulation. Barring that, consider adopting a weekly spray program. (See p. 128 for more information and treatment.)

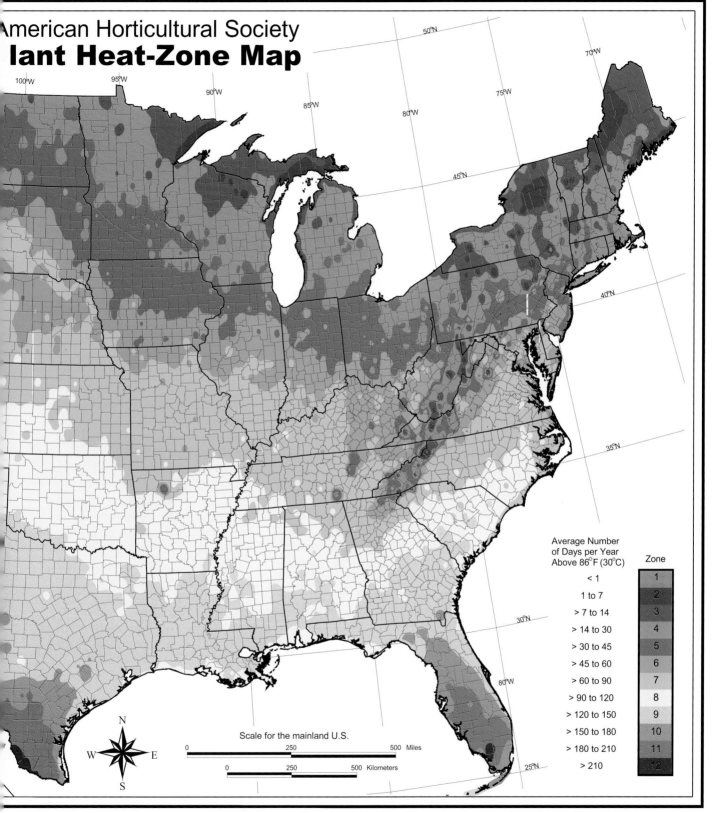

American Horticultural Society
lant Heat-Zone Map

Average Number of Days per Year Above 86°F (30°C)	Zone
< 1	1
1 to 7	2
> 7 to 14	3
> 14 to 30	4
> 30 to 45	5
> 45 to 60	6
> 60 to 90	7
> 90 to 120	8
> 120 to 150	9
> 150 to 180	10
> 180 to 210	11
> 210	12

Scale for the mainland U.S.

The AHS Plant Heat-Zone Map shows 12 zones in the U.S. The zones are based on the number of days above 86° F, when plants begin to experience damage.

Certain microclimates can also produce hot, humid conditions. Low lying south- or west-facing gardens with little breeze are prime breeding grounds for black spot.

SOIL, SOIL TESTING AND SOIL IMPROVEMENT

Knowing the makeup of your soil is crucial to successful gardening. Clockwise from bottom: sand; clay; humus; loam.

Soil is the soul of the garden, literally feeding and invigorating the plants anchored in it. When we think of soil, we generally think of the inorganic mineral matter (clay, silt and sand) that composes roughly half of any given volume of soil. But soil is also composed of organic matter (the more the better), air and water.

Kinds of Soil

Soils are classified by the size of the mineral particles most prevalent. Sand, and in extreme cases, coarse gravel, is the largest particle size. Sand particles are spherical in shape and do not fit well together. Imagine a box full of golf balls—lots of air space and relatively little surface-to-surface contact. Sandy soil is light and easy to work, warms quickly in the spring, drains quickly and is rich in oxygen. Plant roots penetrate easily. However, sandy soil doesn't retain much water or hold many nutrients. Unless well adapted, plants grown in sandy soil need considerable supplemental water and nutrients.

Clay is the smallest particle size, and is plate-like in shape. Imagine pancakes tossed randomly into a box—very little air space and lots of surface-to-surface contact. Clay soil retains moisture and nutrients longer than sandy soil but is also heavy and difficult to work, warms slowly in the spring, drains slowly and has little oxygen.

In the middle of sand and clay is silt. Silt is of medium particle size and shape, possessing properties of both sand and clay.

Loam is the term given to soil with an appropriate balance of clay, silt and sand and a good deal of organic matter. Loam drains well but doesn't dry out too rapidly, is rich in plant nutrients and has plenty of air space. Loam is the ideal garden

SOIL COMPONENTS

1-5% organic matter
25% air
25% water
45% mineral matter

Sandy soil won't form a ball when you squeeze it. Clay soil will stay together.

soil but not all that common. However, repeated applications of organic matter will improve almost any soil. (See the "Soil Improvement" section below.)

Soil Testing

There are two ways to determine the kind of soil in your garden. The quickest way is to take a handful of moist soil in your hand and squeeze it. If it forms a tight ball that doesn't come apart when you tap it, you have a clay soil. Additionally, clay soil is sticky when wet but hard and lumpy when dry. Sandy soil doesn't form much of a ball when moist and it runs through your fingers easily. If your soil holds together when you squeeze it but breaks apart when you tap it, you have loam.

The second, more thorough, way to determine your soil type is to have it tested by your local extension service. Soil testing is easy to do and generally costs less than $10. Contact your county extension service office to find out how to take a soil sample and where to send it. Employees will supply

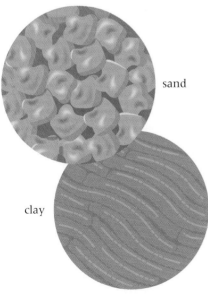

clay   sand

Soil composition: Sand particles are spherical and fit together loosely. Clay is made of tight, plate-shaped particles.

CHARACTERISTICS OF GOOD GARDEN SOIL

- Drains well
- Holds moisture
- Warms early in spring
- Is easily tilled or cultivated
- Is rich in plant nutrients

---

detailed instructions. You'll find the phone number in the county or state listings of your phone book, or a local Master Gardener hotline can help.

Soil test results tell you the kind of soil you have, its pH, the nutrient levels and suggested ways to improve your soil based on the kinds of plants you want to grow. Be sure to tell the extension office that you're growing roses, so it'll test for magnesium, an element roses need for vigorous growth.

Soil Improvement

No matter what kind of soil you have, you can improve it with organic matter. Organic matter is simply decomposed plant and animal matter, but it does magical things for soil. As plants and animals decay, a product called humus is produced. Humus is a sticky substance that causes soil particles to clump together in loose clusters. This is good both for sandy soils that don't stick together at all, and for clay soils that stick together too tightly. The crumbly structure produces passages for air and water to move through and the decaying material adds nutrients to the soil for plant roots to take up. Building soil by adding organic matter is a long-term activity—but vigorous, healthy roses will be your reward!

Fall is an excellent time to add organic matter, prior to fall tilling or digging. In new gardens, cover the entire garden with organic matter—aged manure, compost, leaf mold, peat moss, mushroom compost or cotton burr compost—up to six inches deep. Then till or dig it in as deeply as possible: 8 to 10 inches deep is minimal; 16 to 24 inches is ideal.

Animal manure—cow, horse, chicken and the like—is a popular soil amendment because it improves soil structure and is rich in nutrients. But keep a couple of points in mind when using manure. First, use only old, well-rotted or composted manure. Fresh manure is "hot" and the heat and ammonia produced as it breaks down in the soil will burn plant roots. However, if you live in a colder climate, you could spread fresh manure on dormant beds to decompose over winter, and then dig it in in the spring. Well-rotted manure is odorless and looks like dark soil.

The second point to remember is that manure is relatively high in nitrogen and low in phosphorus, so it often promotes cane and leaf growth at the expense of root growth. For this reason, you might consider adding manure in the fall instead of the spring (when root growth is occurring), or adding phosphorus at the same time manure is added. Because phosphorus is not soluble and does not move through the soil readily, surface applications are much less effective than those that are worked into the soil near plant roots.

If your soil test indicates that magnesium is in short supply, scatter Epsom salts around each plant, up to $1/2$ cup per mature plant. Check your soil annually to see if you need to add more.

Mapping Soil Conditions, pH and Rainfall

Soil Maps

The Natural Resources Conservation Service (NRCS), formerly the Soil Conservation Service, is a USDA agency charged with mapping the soils in the United States. Working hand-in-hand with state agencies, the NRCS takes aerial photos of nearly every county in the United States and produces a soil survey. If you are a landowner you can request a free copy of the soil map for your county.

Soil surveys contain a wealth of information including localized soil information, spring and fall average freeze dates, and temperature and precipitation averages. It is a good way to get a general grasp of the gardening conditions you will encounter in your own backyard.

To locate your property on a soil map it is helpful to know the legal description. If you aren't sure what the legal description of your property is, you might try talking with your mortgage company, because a legal description is required to apply for a mortgage loan.

Soil pH

Soil acidity and alkalinity is measured by a pH factor between 1.0 and 14.0, with 7.0 being neutral. Soil pH affects the availability of nutrients in the soil. Most nutrients are readily available for plants to take up when the soil pH is 6.0 to 7.0.

Soil acidity and alkalinity levels vary greatly across the country, but a few generalizations can be made. Acidic soils generally occur in areas like the Southeast where

Oskaloosa

Kansas River

Martin-Vinland-Sogn association: Deep, moderately well drained, gently sloping to moderately sloping soils.

Pawnee-Martin-Vinland association: Deep, moderately well drained, gently sloping to strongly sloping soils.

Pawnee-Grundy-Shelby association: Deep, nearly level to strongly sloping, well drained to somewhat poorly drained soils.

Kennebec-Wabash-Reading association: Deep, nearly level, well drained to very poorly drained soils.

Eudora-Kimo association: Deep, nearly level to gently undulating, well drained and somewhat poorly drained soils.

Your county soil map can be an invaluable growing guide and help you understand the conditions your plants grow in. On this example, each color represents a different soil type—an important growing factor.

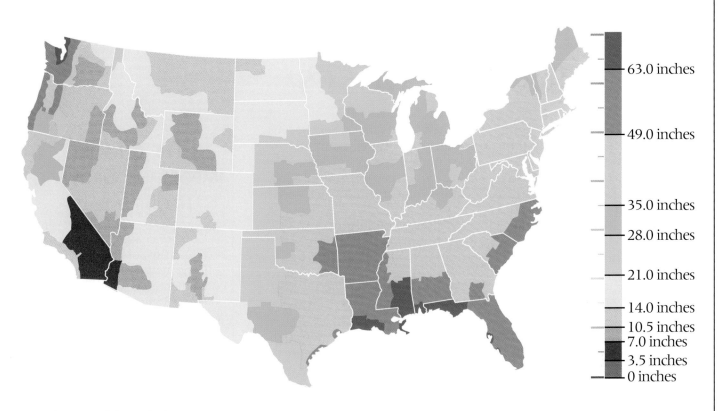

63.0 inches

49.0 inches

35.0 inches
28.0 inches

21.0 inches

14.0 inches
10.5 inches
7.0 inches
3.5 inches
0 inches

Rainfall map of the United States.

rainfall is heavy and soils are sandy and high in organic matter. Areas of western Washington and Oregon and the northern coast of California also tend to be overly acidic. Many plants grow well in slightly acidic soil, including blueberries, rhododendrons, azaleas, camellias and other plants in the heath family. Alkaline soils generally occur in regions with light rainfall and with high levels of calcium in the soil and subsoil.

Most roses prefer a pH between 6.5 and 6.8. If you don't have your soil tested at a lab (which really is the best method), you can purchase an inexpensive soil pH test kit at your local garden center. If your soil pH is lower than 6.5, add dolomitic limestone to increase the alkalinity. One cup of limestone per square yard will raise soil pH one tenth of a point (e.g. 5.8 to 5.9). Scatter it evenly over the soil and work it in two or

three inches deep. Test yearly for changes in pH.

If your soil pH is higher than desired, add iron sulfate or aluminum sulfate to decrease the alkalinity. To lower the soil pH one tenth of a unit, use $^2/_3$ cup aluminum sulfate or $^3/_4$ cup iron sulfate per square yard. Scatter evenly over the soil and work in two or three inches deep.

If you have your soil tested by your state extension office, the test results include pH. The results will tell you how much lime or sulfur to add to bring the pH to the desired level. Again, test annually for changes.

Precipitation

Rainfall and snowfall varies greatly across the country. Nevada averages 4 to 20 inches of precipitation per year. At the opposite extreme, Alabama averages 35 to 64 inches of rainfall per year. Learn your

rainfall amount and seasonal patterns, and select rose classes that grow best with the amount of precipitation that falls naturally.

In general roses are a thirsty bunch and prefer 1 inch of water per week during the growing season. Place a rain gauge in your garden to keep track of the weekly rainfall. If less than 1 inch is falling per week during the growing season, you'll need to supply supplemental water.

On the other hand, roses do not like wet feet. Too much water in the root zone for too long will causes roots to rot, and the plant will die. You can try to combat waterlogged soil by adding organic matter, planting in raised beds and/or installing a drainage system. If you live in a climate with high rainfall and poor soil drainage cannot be corrected, the choice of roses is limited to *R. palustris*, the only rose we know of that tolerates poor drainage.

GROWING REQUIREMENTS; ORDERING AND CHOOSING ROSES

You'll earn great rewards in growing roses if you meet their basic cultural requirements. They are long-lived plants, so it's worth your time and effort to 1) select a site that meets their needs, 2) determine the appropriate classes and cultivars, 3) prepare the soil and 4) plant your roses correctly. In this section, we'll cover the first two topics.

Growing Requirements

In general, roses need 6 hours of sunlight, excellent drainage, and ample water and nutrients. Shelter from strong winds keeps foliage from drying out, and good air circulation reduces disease problems. Roses do not grow well near deeply rooted plants like trees, because there is too much competition for moisture and nutrients. (For this same reason, roses are more vigorous in a weed-free garden.)

Roses grow in most soil types, but do best in a well-drained soil that retains some moisture. Rose roots do not tolerate waterlogged soil for any length of time, nor can they stand drying out. Roses are heavy feeders and grow much better in soil rich in organic matter. The desired pH is between 6.5 and 6.8, although they will tolerate a greater range if ample moisture and nutrients are present. Unless you grow them as individual specimens, roses should be spaced closely enough in the garden so that they merge with each other and with other plants, but not so close that they overlap and become tangled. A garden site that does not provide these conditions may not be an impossible site, but it requires an appropriate choice of rose class and cultivar.

> ## THE 6 MOST IMPORTANT GROWING REQUIREMENTS
>
> - Good drainage
> - 6 hours of sunlight
> - Consistent moisture
> - Nutrient-rich soil
> - Protection from strong wind
> - Good air circulation

Choosing and Ordering Roses

The next step after assessing your garden site and growing conditions, and determining which kinds of roses will grow best in those conditions, is to determine where to get your plants and in what form. Roses can be purchased at your local garden center or through mail-order companies. Each source has advantages and disadvantages.

Mail-order Companies

Mail-order companies are a good bet if

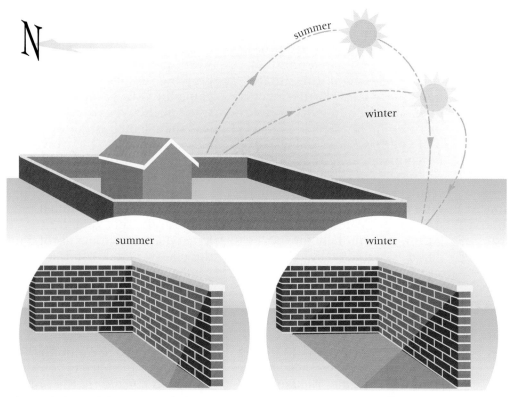

The variations of the sun's path from winter to summer makes a big difference in growing conditions.

In windy areas, a lattice, open-work fence, or loose hedge that breaks up wind currents, may be better than a solid wall that causes damaging downdrafts.

you are looking for harder-to-find roses than your local garden center carries. Mail-order rose sources often specialize in a particular type of rose; for example, antique roses, fragrant roses or super-hardy roses. The best of these companies have very informative catalogs and are often helpful on the telephone. Mail-order companies ship at the best planting time for your area. That is usually early spring for cold winter climates, fall for mild winter climates and winter for very warm climates.

The main disadvantage to buying from a mail-order source is that you can only get plants at the time designated for delivery to your region of the country. If you live in Oklahoma and want to plant roses in June, you're pretty much out of luck until the next spring. The other disadvantage is that you can't inspect the plants prior to purchase. You have to rely on the integrity of the mail-order company to provide good-quality plants. Unfortunately, in some cases this doesn't happen. Yet as in most any business, the vast majority of companies are reputable and stand behind their product. Read their guarantee and discuss what you want on the phone before you place your order.

To avoid disappointment, talk with other gardeners in your

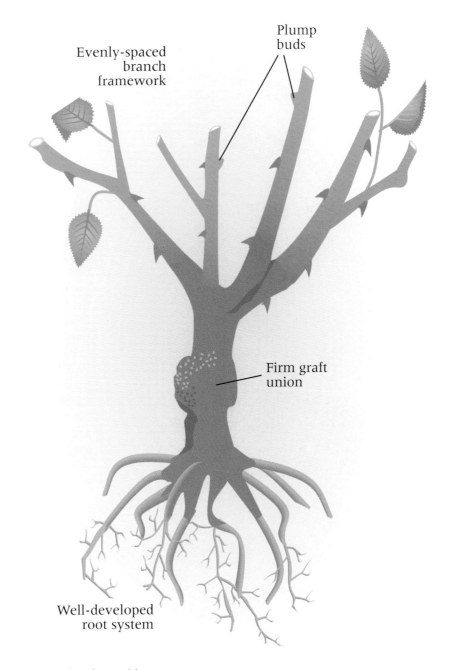

Characteristics of a good bare-root rose.

Evenly-spaced branch framework

Plump buds

Firm graft union

Well-developed root system

area or members of your local American Rose Society chapter to get recommendations. You can also try placing a small order with a firm you are unfamiliar with, then ordering in larger quantities the next year if you are pleased with the product.

Plants shipped by mail are usually "bare-root," meaning there is no soil around the roots. Be sure you are ordering from a source that offers **dormant, 2-year-old, grade #1** roses. A #1 rose will be at least 18 inches tall (15 inches for

Gently tease away the roots of a potbound plant.

Floribundas) and will have at least three vigorous canes. These are good-sized plants that should establish quickly in your garden. Lesser grades (#1$^{1}/_{2}$ and #2) are cheaper, but are usually weaker plants and should be avoided.

Local Retailers

Local nurseries and garden centers are the alternative to mail-order sources. One advantage of shopping locally is that you can personally select your plants, ensuring that only vigorous roses make it to your garden. The second advantage is that you can usually buy roses during most of the growing season—not just early spring. The disadvantage is that the selection, especially of harder-to-find varieties, is usually not great. And you'll often find that the varieties being offered are not necessarily the best for your climate.

In very early spring you might find bare-root roses at your local retailer. As the season progresses, you'll find only potted roses. Potted

roses can be planted in the garden at almost any time the ground is not frozen, although in hotter climates mid-summer planting is not recommended due to heat extremes and the negative effect on immature plants.

Buy plants that are grown in large containers. Number 1 roses should be potted in a 2-gallon container or larger. Avoid smaller container sizes—the roots are either small to begin with or have been pruned severely and will not develop well after planting.

If you buy roses locally, look for the following signs of health:

- Thick, sturdy canes without bruising or cracks.
- The pith (interior) of the canes should be firm and white. If the pith is brown, the cane is dead.
- Good leaf color.
- Freedom from disease and insects. Check under the leaves and along the stem for signs of pests.
- Good, healthy roots. Gently remove the plant from the pot to check its roots. Thick, white roots with no black areas should be emerging at the edge of the rootball.
- Examine the structure of the plant.
  - The center should be open.
  - The canes should be pruned so that three to five evenly spaced canes grow out from the center of the plant.
  - All the canes should be thick and have three to five actively growing buds.

Some local retailers, mainly grocery stores and hardware stores, carry roses packaged in boxes or bags. The canes of these roses are often sealed in wax to prevent them from drying out, and the roots are severely pruned to fit in the packaging. If you decide to purchase roses this way it is best to buy them very early in the season or not at all. Cut away and discard the bag or box and soak the entire plant, roots and canes, in a bucket of water for 24 hours. Then prune canes back to near the bud union and plant as you would a bare-root rose.

Own-root and Grafted Roses

Commercial nurserymen grow roses in one of two ways. Grafted roses have a below-ground rootstock that's different from the above-ground cultivar. Grafted roses have a noticeable bulge called the bud union at the bottom of the stem. This is where the hybrid variety has been grafted onto a rootstock with vigorous root growth. Rose propagators do this because the roots of grafted roses grow very quickly, in turn causing the above-ground portion of the plant to grow quickly. This is not necessarily a good thing for the gardener! If the upper portion of the plant is winterkilled back to the bud union, the canes that reemerge will not be the desired cultivar. They will be shoots from the underground rootstock and will bear less attractive—and certainly different—foliage and flowers.

Own-root roses are the same plant on top and bottom. If the top of an own-root rose winterkills to the ground, the resprouting canes will be exactly like the original desired cultivar. Own-root roses may be a little smaller in the pot and a little slower to establish in the garden than grafted roses, but they're far better plants in the long run. Unfortunately, own-root roses are not as common as grafted plants. There are no own-root Hybrid Teas, for example. Mail-order rose specialists often have a good selection of own-root Rugosa and old-fashioned roses.

Climbing Miniature 'Jeanne Lajoie' in a mixed garden setting.

PREPARING AND DIGGING YOUR BED

While it's true that some roses aren't terribly particular about the condition of the soil from which they spring (such as some of the Old Garden Roses and Rugosas), all roses will benefit if you take the time to make a proper home for them before inviting them to your garden. It's literally digging a path to greater garden glory.

The greatest considerations for site selection and preparation are sunlight (at least 6 hours of sunlight), ability of air to circulate among and through the garden, and adequate drainage. Roses don't like damp feet! Be sure to select a location where your roses do not have to compete with neighboring trees or large shrubs for sunlight, water or nutrients. Also

find a site where harsh drying winds won't be a factor in your roses' health.

Plan Ahead for Timely Planting

It's also best if you've planned ahead. Select the site and prepare the bed 3 to 4 months before setting out your plants, giving the soil time to settle. Fall preparation for springtime planting is a good idea, especially for areas with a lot of precipitation in late winter and early spring. Roses prefer slightly acidic soil (pH 6.5 to 6.8). It's a good idea to have your soil tested (contact your county extension agent for help with this); from this evaluation you can either add sulfur to make your soil more acidic, or ground limestone to raise the pH. Your extension agent can recommend the appropriate rate of application to bring the pH of your soil up or down (or see page 97 for another pH-adjusting formula).

How big a space do you need to prepare? Plan on digging an area $2^1/2$ to 3 feet in diameter per plant. This will give their roots plenty of room to stretch out as they establish themselves in your garden.

Drainage Counts

Once you've selected a sunny spot for your new roses, evaluate the site's drainage. Soil with a swampy character or high clay content does not drain well, and requires extra planning. You can go to a bit of trouble and install a trench drain, in which you bury drain tile (pipe with holes in it) 18 to 20 inches below ground level. Surround the pipe (drain holes pointing toward the sky) with

Plants will not thrive without proper preparation of the planting area. By working the soil and digging in any amendments your roses will need, you help ensure their success—and your ultimate enjoyment.

'Alchymist' trained on an arbor transforms this quiet garden setting.

several chopped up banana peels (which are high in potassium) to the soil of rose beds. Mix the topsoil from the tarp back into the excavated area, then blend it all together well. If you're building a raised bed or terrace, proceed as above, although you can reduce the depth to which you first excavate to 12 inches or so.

Install the sides or walls of the structure, and then fill the bed with a mixture of equal parts topsoil and organic matter along with some sharp sand, as recommended earlier.

A Happy Home for Each Plant

Once you have prepared your site and given it time to settle, you're now ready to dig holes for your specific plants. Again, it's handy to have a tarp spread out next to your site on which you can pile the soil you're digging out of the hole. For bare-root plants, dig a hole 16 to 18 inches wide and 12 inches to 18 inches deep and then build a mound of soil in the center of the hole over which you will spread the plant's roots. As you're building the mound, be sure to press down firmly with your hands to eliminate air pockets in the soil. For container-grown plants, dig a hole the same depth as the container and at least 18 inches wide.

coarse gravel, and angle the pipe down and away from the site to carry excess water away from the bed.

An easier solution is to build a raised bed (or several smaller ones) which extend 16 to 24 inches above the surrounding soil level. You can build the sides from a variety of materials, depending on your budget and how permanent you want your beds: stone, cedar, redwood, brick or even hard plastic. When sizing your beds, be sure you can reach the center easily.

A sloped site provides good drainage, but can be prone to soil erosion. If your slope is abrupt enough to cause rain trenches, create a series of terraces to take advantage of the drainage while providing stable sites for your roses.

Building Good Soil

Whether you're building a raised bed, a terrace or a site level with surrounding ground, start by removing the sod from the site (either transplant it to a bare spot in the yard or add it to your compost pile). Then dig the area to a depth of 16 to 20 inches. The best method is to spread a tarp adjacent to the site you're preparing, removing the first 8 to 10 inches of topsoil and piling it on the tarp. Then dig down into the next 8 to 10 inches, loosening the soil and adding organic matter (up to 50 percent by volume). Leaf mold, well-rotted manure or peat moss are good for this, along with about 10 percent by volume of sharp sand.

Mix in any amendments required to adjust your soil's pH, and include a handful of gypsum if your soil has a high clay content. Add rock phosphate or superphosphate at the rate recommended on the package to stimulate root vigor, along with a bucket of spent coffee grounds (these improve drainage and add acidity) and

PLANTING TECHNIQUES

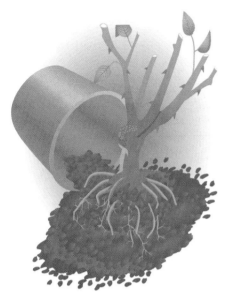

If a potted rose's roots are too new to hold soil, plant it as a bare-root rose.

PLANTING TIME FOR BARE-ROOT ROSES	
Minimum Winter Temperature	**Planting Time**
Above 10°F	Whenever dormant plants are available.
Between 10°F and -10°F	Early spring or late fall.
Below -10°F	Early spring.

Planting Time and Holding Containerized Roses

Roses purchased in containers can be planted at any time your garden soil is not frozen. As mentioned previously, it's best not to plant during extreme mid-summer heat. If heat pre-vents planting, or if soil is too wet, containerized roses can be held until planting conditions improve. Simply place the pot in an area protected from hot mid-day sun and drying wind, and keep the soil moist.

Planting Time and Holding Bare-root Roses

Planting time for bare-root roses varies according to the severity of your winter weather. If temperatures stay above 10°F, you can plant whenever dormant roses are available. If minimum winter temperatures stay between 10°F and -10°F, plant bare-root roses in early spring or late fall. If winter tempera-tures drop below -10°F, plant only in the spring.

After you receive bare-root roses they should be planted as soon as the weather permits. Bare-root plants should be dormant (plants that have not leafed out) when you receive them from a mail-order source or purchase them locally. Bare-root plants will often be dried out when they arrive. If they will be planted the same day they arrive or the next day, soak the roots in a bucket of water. Do not soak plants unless they can be planted promptly, and do not soak for more than 24 hours.

If your roses can't be planted within 24 hours of arrival, moist-en the packing material and repack the plants. Keep them in a cool area (but above freezing). An unheated garage usually works well. Plants can be held 2 or 3 days this way.

If they must be held longer, you should "heel them in" out-doors. The goal is to keep plants from breaking dormancy until they are planted in the garden. There are two ways to do this, depending on the number of plants. If you have only two or three plants, they can be grouped together in a 5-gallon bucket. Fill the bucket with loose material like sphag-

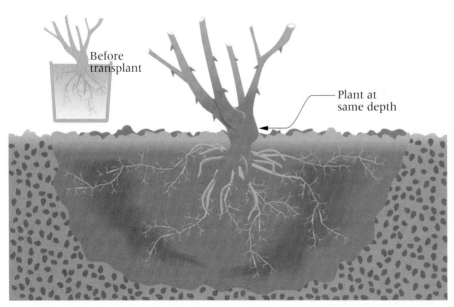

Before transplant

Plant at same depth

Plant own-root roses at the same depth, or slightly deeper, than their depth in the container.

PLANTING DEPTH FOR GRAFTED ROSES

Winter Climate	Planting Depth
Mild winter (Zones 7 and above)	Graft union at soil level
Severe winter (Zones 6 and below)	Graft union 2″ below soil level

Mound soil over an above-ground bud union to protect your new plant.

num peat moss, perlite or sawdust, and then water them. Be sure that water is not standing in the bottom of the bucket or the plants will rot. Then place

the bucket in a cool area above freezing.

If you have larger quantities of plants, lay them in a shallow trench—about 6 inches deep—and cover the roots and bud union (if present) with soil. If the tops are dried out or if you have strong winds, place the whole plant in the trench sideways and bury it until you can plant. Plant at the very first opportunity. Heeled-in roses can easily start growing roots before they are permanently planted. The

fewer roots disturbed at planting the better!

Planting Containerized Roses

If the nursery did not prune your roses properly, you'll need to do so prior to planting. Remove dead canes and poorly positioned canes. Cut the rose back so that the center of the plant is open, and three to five strong canes are spaced evenly around the center. Cut canes to the proper height so they have three to five buds per cane. (See the pruning section starting on page 114.)

If you're planting several roses, it's best to prepare the whole planting area as described on pp. 102–103. If you are planting two or three roses, prepare individual planting holes as described on page 103. Either way, dig the hole at least 18 inches wide. It is very important not to crowd roots in a small hole.

Own-root roses should be planted at the same depth they originally grew or slightly deeper.

The depth of the planting hole for *grafted roses* depends on the severity of your winters. In mild-winter climates (temperatures above 10°F), grafted roses should be planted with the bud union at or just below ground level. In severe-winter climates (temperatures below 10°F), the bud union should be planted 2 inches below ground. This helps protect the bud union from severe winter freezes, and helps discourage the rootstock from

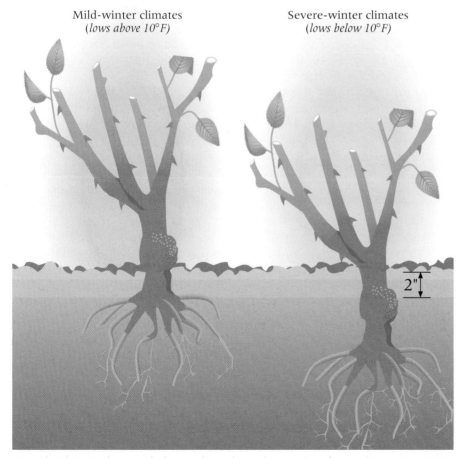

Mild-winter climates
(*lows above 10°F*)

Severe-winter climates
(*lows below 10°F*)

2″

How deeply you plant grafted roses depends on the severity of your climate in winter.

Planting roses that are well established in pots:

1) Dig a big enough hole! A little deeper than the container and at least 6 inches wider all around.

2) Slide the plant out or cut the container. Don't pull it by the stem. Loosen the roots if they're potbound.

3) Plant the rose with the bud union at the right height for your climate (see chart on page 105). Spread the roots out. Fill up the hole loosely. Water thoroughly. Refill the hole with soil.

4) Build a ring of soil around the hole. Water thoroughly again. Water as needed until your rose is established in its new home.

sending up undesirable suckers. If the bud union is below soil level, it's especially important that your soil be well drained.

Containers

Roses are grown in various kinds of containers. Plastic and metal containers, called "cans" by nurserymen, should be cut down the side prior to removing the rose. If the rose is grown in a metal can, your retailer should have shears and can cut the can open when you purchase the plant. Regular garden pruners will cut open plastic pots.

Fiber pots or heavy peat pots are another kind of container used for roses. The common advice on these is to break open the bottom of the fiber pot and to trim the top of it level with the rootball. Then plant the rose in the ground with the fiber pot intact. The better method is to cut the fiber pot on four sides and gently remove the plant.

The roots of container-grown plants will usually be one of two ways. If the rose is newly potted, the root system will not be well developed and soil will fall away from the roots easily when the plant is removed from the pot. If this is the case, wash the soil away gently and plant as if bare-root (see page 104).

If the rose has been potted for some time, the root system will be well developed and the soil ball will stay intact when the pot is removed. In fact, the root system may be so well developed that the plant has become potbound with masses of roots on the outside of the rootball. Potbound roots must be teased away or cut from the rootball so that new roots will grow out into surrounding garden soil.

Once the rose is removed from the container place it gently in

the planting hole with the rootball intact. Be sure the bud union is at the correct depth for your climate and fill the hole loosely with soil. Water and let the soil settle, then finish filling the hole with soil and water again.

If the graft union is above ground, it's a good idea to cover it with soil to prevent dehydration during the first few weeks. Seal pruning cuts on canes with non-toxic wood glue to keep out stem borers.

Planting Bare-root Roses

After your bare-root roses have been soaked in a bucket of water for up to 24 hours, dead canes and poorly positioned canes should be removed if the nursery did not do so. Cut the rose back to three to five canes with three to five buds per cane as described for containerized roses (see the illustration on page 99). Prune off excessively long roots and dead or damaged roots. Be sure to keep the roses in water until the moment you are ready to plant. Drying out, even for a short time, can be fatal.

Dig a planting hole large enough to accommodate all the roots remaining on the plant. You don't want to crowd rose roots in too small a space. Build a soil cone and set the rose on top of it, spreading roots evenly over the cone and downward.

Position grafted roses so that the bud union is at the proper depth for your climate. Hang on to the rose with one hand and backfill the hole, firmly packing the soil in place. Water thoroughly and let the soil settle, then finish filling the hole and water again.

If the graft union is above ground, it's a good idea to cover it with soil to prevent dehydration during the first few weeks. Seal pruning cuts on canes with non-toxic wood glue to keep out stem borers, and remove the metal or paper tag from the plant to keep it from girdling the plant as the cane grows. (If you want to label your plants, use a marker that sticks in the soil.)

Care After Planting

If you enriched the planting bed, or worked nutrients into the planting hole prior to planting, you shouldn't have to feed your roses at planting time. You will need to pay close attention to watering the first season. You'll probably need to water newly planted roses two to three times as often as established roses. Mulch will help conserve soil moisture and keep the roots cooler, but it isn't a substitute for water.

Care for Established Roses

The general rule of thumb for watering established roses is 1 inch of water per week during the growing season. Roses in sandy, fast-draining soil will need to be watered more fre-

Near a wall, leave at least 2 feet between the plant and the support. Train the roots away from the support so they don't suffer in the "rain shadow."

A BONE TO PICK: IGNORE BONE MEAL

Bone meal used to be a good source of slow-acting, long-lasting phosphorus. It still could be; however, we cannot recommend it for two reasons.

First, there's a possibility that it could carry a form of "mad cow disease." While some think that the odds of this are slim in the United States, scientists at the Centers for Disease Control have stated that they cannot guarantee that bone meal poses no risk in this regard. Remember, we rose gardeners get stuck a lot by thorns and get small wounds that could let bone meal dust enter our systems. Is it worth the risk?

A second reason is that nowadays bone meal is processed at much higher temperatures (usually steamed) than before, which neutralizes the effects of the phosphorus.

quently. Plants in heavier clay soil might need to be watered less frequently. The soil should be constantly moist—but not wet—while plants are growing. Keep the bed free of weeds to reduce competition for water and nutrients. Again, mulch your roses!

Fertilizing Established Plants

Roses are heavy feeders and will need additional fertilizer even if planted in soil rich in organic matter. A combination of organic and inorganic fertilizers often provides the best results. An inorganic fertilizer high in phosphorus (5-10-5) will provide quick-acting, concentrated nutrition. An organic fertilizer— such as aged manure —will be longer-lasting and will help build the soil.

Inorganic fertilizer in the form of granular fertilizer should be applied in spring after the danger of a severe freeze is past. Spread the fertilizer evenly around the plants and scratch it into the soil surface prior to a rain or before watering. Follow label directions for specific amounts, but generally, when a complete fertilizer is used, apply 3 pounds per 100 square feet or 1 heaping tablespoon per plant. Applications should be repeated every 6 weeks until July or August, depending on your climate. (You want to reduce fertility early enough that plants have plenty of time to harden off before winter.)

Such organic fertilizers as aged manure or compost (the gardener's "black gold") can be spread on the surface of the soil, then worked in 2 to 3 inches deep, or left to work itself into the soil either in spring or fall. For specific elements, liquid fish emulsion is an organic source of immediately available nitrogen as well as other elements. For phosphorus, use a heaping tablespoon of rock phosphate or colloidal phosphate per plant (but not bone meal—see above). Greensand, wood ashes (not charcoal) and kelp meal are organic sources of potassium. Epsom salts can be used to supply magnesium; scatter up to $1/2$ cup around each mature plant.

SUPPORTS: CLIMBERS AND RAMBLERS

'Blaze' and 'Red Fountain' give a tremendous display when they climb high into a tree.

Climber	Rambler
Larger flowers borne singly or in loose clusters; usually flower on new growth.	Smaller flowers in dense clusters; usually bloom on old wood.
Stiff, very long canes; not as many canes emerging from the crown.	Supple shoots, shorter growing; many new shoots from the base.
Continuous or repeat bloom.	Bloom one time per season, usually mid-summer.
Examples: Noisettes, Cl. Teas, Cl. Hybrid Tea, Modern Climbers.	Examples: Multiflora Hybrids, *R. wichuraiana* Hybrids.

Climbing roses serve a multitude of design purposes in the garden. Climbing roses can beautifully mask an unattractive structure like an old shed, or help soften stark architectural lines like concrete walls. Roses grown on an arbor can help define an entrance or a passageway from one space to another. They can frame a view or provide a vertical focal point in what might otherwise be a dull, horizontal landscape. They are tremendous for breaking up long expanses of fence and for pro-

Secure climbing roses to supports with sturdy materials such as twine. Check your binding materials regularly for fraying.

viding privacy. In addition to all these practical matters, climbing roses bring a touch of romance, maturity and fragrance to the garden.

Kinds of Climbing Roses

Climbing roses are divided into two primary groups: Climbers and Ramblers. Within each of these primary divisions are numerous subgroups. Climbers include Noisettes, Climbing Tea roses, Climbing Hybrid Teas, Modern Climbers and a few other sorts. Ramblers include Multiflora Hybrids, *R. wichuraiana* Hybrids and others. Although each of these groups and subgroups is discussed on pp. 43–45, it is helpful to review the general characteristics of the two primary groups to better understand their garden uses.

Uses for Climbers and Ramblers

Because of their differing growth habits, Climbers and Ramblers are naturally suited to different uses in the garden and to different kinds of support systems.

Climber Uses

Climbers, with their stiff, upright canes, have a natural

affinity for smaller gardens and for relatively formal uses. They are excellent trained against walls and fences, around pillars and on arbors and pergolas. Taller Climbers can be grown into trees. Winter hardiness varies greatly within Climber subgroups so it is important to pick varieties that are adapted to your climate.

Rambler Uses

With the Ramblers' propensity for sprawling growth and pliant stems, they are at home in larger spaces and less formal garden schemes. Ramblers are perfect for growing up and over fences, old stumps and less-than-handsome

As Climbers grow, fasten them where they need extra support.

Vigorous Climber canes need plenty of support.

trees. They are good sprawling shrubs and will readily cover large, unattractive objects or a wood tripod placed in a planting of mixed shrubs. Ramblers are very hardy and disease-free, but tend to get powdery mildew if air circulation is not adequate.

Supporting Structures for Climbers and Ramblers

Climbing roses do not have tendrils, aerial roots or disc-like suction cups. Nor do they twine to attach themselves to a support. Large thorns on some varieties help hook plants into whatever they are growing on, but most must be physically attached to a supportive structure. There are many different ways to provide support for climbing roses. Let your garden

style and budget be your guide.

Walls

To grow a rose against a wall, you need to use a system of wires or a trellis. Wire can be fixed to a wall with eye screws, sometimes called "vine eyes." Stretch wire horizontally between the vine eyes at 12-inch intervals. Keep the wire 1 inch away from the wall. Do this by inserting vine eyes every 3 feet along the length of the wire. Loosely tie main shoots horizontally to the wire with soft twine. If possible, zigzag shoots back and forth to discourage strong upward growth. Some roses have a stiff upright growth habit and can not be trained laterally. Train these in a fan shape.

If you choose to use a trellis against a wall, insert 1-inch spacers between the trellis and the wall to allow good air circulation. Hinging the

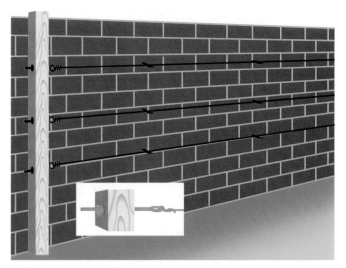

Climbers and Ramblers need strong support and air circulation. On a solid wall or fence, use a system of wires held by vine eyes.

Eyehooks and plastic ties train a rose to a brick wall.

trellis allows painting and maintenance of the wall later without destroying the plant.

A wall provides a warmer (and drier) microclimate than open garden sites, so it might provide a good site for growing some of the less hardy Climbers. Planting directions are the same for roses

When planting a Climber against a wall, angle the top of the plant toward the wall.

2 feet

To provide air space, use long eye screws when fastening roses to a wall or trellis.

'Claire Jacquier', a Noisette, trained on a trellis at the Huntington Botanical Gardens in San Marino, California.

A trellis covered by 'Sparrieshoop'.

grown against walls as for other roses, with one exception. When setting your rose in the planting hole, angle the top of the canes back toward the wall and feather the roots out away from the wall (page 107); remember that walls cast a rain shadow and the ground around a wall will be drier than in open sites. Be sure to incorporate plenty of mois-

'Reine des Violettes' trained on an entryway support.

ture-retaining organic matter and to water deeply as needed.

Pillars, Arbors, Pergolas, Arches, Tripods

As you consider building or buying a structure to support roses, remember that Climbing and, especially, Rambling roses are very vigorous and can easily collapse a flimsy support with their weight. Upright posts, poles or pillars should be at least 4 inches thick, no more than 6 feet apart and sunk into the ground at least 2 feet. Cross members should not be thinner than 2 inches. Treated lumber will last longer than non-treated lumber.

Another support method uses posts and wire, ropes or chains. Set posts, at least 4 inches thick, no more than 10 feet apart and 2 feet in the ground. Corner posts should have additional brace posts added. Stretch heavy wire, rope or chain from post to post at 12-inch intervals and train roses across the lateral supports.

When training a rose on a pillar or lamp post, spiral the stems around the support.

If you grow roses on pillars or lamp posts, spiral strong shoots around the post and anchor them to the post. This will encourage flowering lateral shoots.

Tripods, sometimes called "tuteurs," are a great way to support Ramblers. They can be made to any height and placed singly or in groups in a mixed shrub border.

Trees and Shrubs

Smaller trees and shrubs past their prime are natural supports for Ramblers. Non-productive, old fruit trees become glorious when covered with Ramblers. Climbing roses are better suited to tall trees as they often grow to 30 feet.

After amending soil properly, place the rose 2 feet away from the base of the supporting tree or shrub. When deciding on which side of the tree to plant, consider both the prevailing winds and sunlight. Ideally, you want your rose to be blown toward the tree rather than away and you want it on the side receiving the most sunlight.

Angle your rose toward the tree or shrub and tie the two loosely together. You may need to use bamboo poles to bridge the gap between the rose and the tree or shrub. As your rose grows, it will not need to be tied again. Pay close attention to

Leave room for air circulation by using batten strips between a trellis and a wall.

'Rhonda' on a rustic support makes an excellent bower.

watering and fertilization, especially if your supporting plant is still alive and taking moisture and nutrients from the soil.

It may take several years before a rose grown through a tree blooms because it needs to emerge into bright sunlight before flowering well.

Pruning Climbers and Ramblers

Wait 2 or 3 years after planting a Climber before pruning. You can remove dead and weak growth as needed prior to that time.

After the initial waiting period, prune Climbing roses to

encourage new shoots from the crown of the plant and to promote flowering. Do a very light annual pruning of everblooming Climbers in early spring. Simply cut back the lateral shoots that flowered the previous year to two or three buds. The best flowers are produced on laterals growing from 2- or 3-year-old vertical canes.

Do heavier pruning after the first flush of flowers, usually late June or early July. Prune out old, woody, upright canes that are not producing blooms any more. When you cut out an old cane, select a vigorous new shoot to train to take its place, then remove the remainder of the unwanted shoots at the base.

Do not cut back long canes unless they are too long for the allotted space or they are not healthy. If canes are growing in the wrong direction, try to retrain them prior to removing them. If you do have to remove long canes, it is best to take them out in sections so that you don't damage newer growth when the old cane is pulled out of the plant.

'Zéphirine Drouhin' on a tall iron support.

Rambling roses should be pruned in very early spring. Cut old or dead stems to the ground. As new shoots emerge and grow, train them into position.

Planting and staking a standard rose.

Dig a hole at least 2 feet wide and insert the stake firmly.

The stake should be a foot or so taller than the rose's trunk.

Fill in the hole, water well, and fasten the trunk to the stake with rubber-coated wiring or tree ties.

MULCHING

The Great Cover-up

Mulching is a process of nature. Look at the leaf covering on the forest floor which holds moisture and puts nutrients back into the soil. Look at the mat of needles protecting the ground under a pine tree. By adding protective material, we follow nature's example in our own gardens.

Mulching your roses is absolutely essential. Here's why:

- *Controls soil temperature.* Mulch moderates soil and root temperatures. In hot weather, mulch keeps soil (and roots) cooler. In cold weather, it keeps them warmer.
- *Keeps down weeds.* Weeds compete for water and nutrients. Weeds that sprout through mulch are easier to pull. Constant cultivation, on the other hand, takes time, makes your back ache, and brings weed seeds to the light, where they sprout.
- *Conserves moisture.* Mulch prevents evaporation from the soil surface. It also absorbs rainfall that might otherwise run off.
- *Helps prevent disease.* Many rose diseases are caused by contact with soil- or water-borne organisms. Mulch makes water trickle instead of splash. It creates a barrier between soil and leaf.
- *Aids soil structure.* Mulch prevents soil from compacting and crusting.
- *Adds nutrients.* Mulch adds organic matter to the soil, which improves nutrition. Old mulch can be turned in to the soil, or used to boost compost.
- *Makes your garden more attractive.* Mulch can be an attractive visual feature, providing a contrast element and a uniform backdrop for your rose garden. You can even enhance the color impact of your flowers with it.
- *Controls traffic.* In high-traffic areas, mulch acts as a visual border and marks your "keep off" areas. As such, it also helps prevent you from getting too close to your roses with the lawn mower and string trimmer.

Is There Ever a Time When You Wouldn't Mulch Your Roses?

Just a few:

- *When your soil needs to warm up or dry up.* Don't apply mulch too early; let the sun and wind do their jobs first.
- *In a bed newly planted with seeds of companion plants.* Wait for the seedlings to get big enough before applying mulch.
- *If your soil retains so much moisture that plants may rot.* If that's the case, work in organic matter or use raised beds or containers. Then mulch!

Roses spaced to allow air circulation, and mulched to conserve moisture.

MULCHING CONTAINER-GROWN ROSES

When you grow roses in containers, mulch is doubly important. First, containers dry out more quickly than do beds. In hotter weather, unmulched container plants will quickly dry out and the plants will suffer from heat stress. Second, containers can get very hot in the mid-day sun, and stress the feeder roots near the pot's sides.

So by all means, lay a surface mulch on your container roses, just as on your beds. But when you plant, leave 3 or 4 inches between the top of the container and the surface of the soil. Two inches of space are for your moisture-conserving mulch and the other inch or two is to let water collect.

Here's another way to use mulch to keep roots cooler: Place your potted rose inside a larger container, one that leaves at least an inch in between the two pots. Fill the air space with a mulch—vermiculite, moss, pebbles, just about anything that insulates. Your inner container will be cooler, and your rose happier.

The Best Rose Mulches

Everything from stones to newspaper to sea kelp can be used as mulching materials. Here are the best rose mulches:

- *Cocoa shells.* Attractive dark-brown shells make some lighter roses look better. The shells absorb (and thus retain) water, but if they get dry, they can blow away.

- *Compost.* Black gold that's good for everything garden-related. Don't work it in to the soil; let the worms do that. If you want, cover it with chopped leaves, straw or other mulch materials. If you can't make enough, buy it from your municipality or garden center.
- *Corn gluten.* Add to mulch mix. It's a weed inhibitor and a source of nutrition.
- *Leafmold.* Shredded, chopped or composted leaves are a good mulch and look good too.
- *Manure (composted).* Slowly feeds the soil and the plant; looks good, too. Keep it from directly touching stems, though.
- *Mushroom soil.* This by-product of the mushroom industry is dark and earthy.
- *Pine bark.* If composted, it gives a great appearance to the bed. If chunky, it lasts longer and makes it harder for slugs to maneuver. Lowers pH a little.

- *Pine needles.* They add a little acidity to the soil, last long and look nice. Add some straw or shredded leaves to them for added bulk.
- *Salt marsh hay.* This seaside product lasts a long time. Be sure that it's been washed up on shore, not harvested (harvesting is bad environmentally).
- *Straw.* It's plentiful and looks good. Mixes well with other materials too.
- *Wood bark, chips and shavings.* Bagged or bulk, such woods as fir, cedar, cypress or redwood are attractive, long-lasting mulches. It's tempting to get free or cheap fresh chips from tree-trimming companies or city utilities, but beware of two things: 1) They need nitrogen to break down, so add compost, aged manure or other nitrogen fertilizer first. 2) Don't use chips of diseased trees. You could spread the disease to your nearby trees.

Mulch Materials to Avoid
- *Bleached cardboard.* Leaches toxins.
- *Black walnut, walnut or pecan hulls.* Too tannic for most plants.
- *Fresh grass clippings.* They mat, then they rot. Dry them first and add to chopped leaves, needles or other mulches; or compost them.
- *Hay.* It would be great if it wasn't full of seeds that sprout. If it's spoiled hay, go ahead and use it; the seeds won't be a problem.
- *Whole leaves.* Will mat and act as a barrier. Chop them with the lawn mower, throw them into a shredder or compost them.
- *Fresh manure.* Too "hot"; will burn roots. Don't forget the aroma, too! Compost it or let it age for a few months first.
- *Sawdust.* Will take nitrogen from the soil as it decomposes. Compost it or mix it in with other materials, in which case you should add some nitrogen fertilizer on top of the soil before you apply it.

Mulching Is Easy
Keep these ideas in mind when you mulch your roses:
- *Wait for the soil to warm up.*
- *Apply 3 to 6 inches of mulch.* Use enough to keep weeds from sprouting.
- *Cultivate the soil lightly to begin with, so there's no layer of hard earth.* Avoid stepping directly on the soil and compacting it. Use a square board to distribute your weight evenly if necessary.
- *Replenish your mulch as it decomposes.* Work the old mulch in or compost it.
- *Keep mulch from actually touching your rose stems.* Leave 2 to 4 inches of air space around stems for circulation.

MULCH AND CRITTERS

- *Mice.* Some folks say that mulch attracts mice. If you've got a lot of mice, mulch isn't the cause of your problem. Instead of not using mulch, get or borrow a cat, or set traps!
- *Slugs and Snails.* In some climates slugs and snails like to live and slither around in the cool atmosphere of a mulched garden. They can eat leaves and damage a rose bush. There are poisonous baits in the form of pellets, but they won't work when wet, and birds may eat them, so we can't recommend them. If you need to get rid of slimy slugs and snails, here are four techniques to try.
  1. Trap them under boards or grapefruit halves. In the morning, drop your harvest into soapy water to take care of them for good.
  2. Use stale beer or water and yeast in shallow dishes. Attracted by the scent of yeast, the pests will slide in and drown.
  3. Use copper strips around your plants. It's said that this gives the pests a mild shock.
  4. Lay down horticultural-grade diatomaceous earth (DE) or ground-up oyster shells, which will cut their soft underbellies.

There are good critters who like mulch, too.
- *Earthworms.* Worms like cooler soil. If it's too hot, they'll dig down to the subsoil. Mulch encourages worms to work in your plants' main root zone.

EASY PRUNING AND MAINTENANCE

A newly pruned Hybrid Tea with just a few strong canes.

Does the thought of growing roses instill fear in your heart—fear of lots of pruning and lots of rules? Fear not! It's not that hard. You gain pruning expertise simply by doing it. Any mistakes are quickly mended by new growth, giving you many more opportunities in coming seasons to enjoy a rose plant with a pleasing shape and an abundance of flowers.

While rosarians have proposed numerous guidelines for pruning over the years, the best pruning advice will be your

Close-up of a newly pruned Hybrid Tea showing proper pruning angle and height.

own, derived from your experience with the specific varieties you've chosen and the climate in which you garden. But there are some general guidelines to follow.

Pruning for Profit

Most roses benefit from pruning, whether it be simple removal of dead wood or more involved trimming and shaping. You want to prune your roses to keep them healthy by removing unproductive and damaged canes (which are prone to disease). Additionally, your roses need good air circulation to keep diseases at bay. Pruning can open up a plant to improve circulation and light penetration. You can also improve the shape of the plant itself so that it's pleasing in your garden setting. Finally, pruning affects the size and number of subsequent blossoms.

When planting roses in your garden, it is best to shape them up at planting time, and

then leave them pretty much alone until they reach mature size (2 or 3 years), removing only dead wood and damaged canes before then.

Timing Is Everything

Modern Shrub roses and repeat-blooming Old Roses benefit from pruning—whether light or severe—in early spring, just as they are breaking dormancy. Unless you garden in the South where late frosts are not a problem, you want to avoid pruning too early, because pruning triggers new growth which is very susceptible to late frosts. Alternatively, you don't want to prune too late; the energy that the plant expends on producing unwanted new growth is lost to the plant for the season. In warm-winter climates, gardeners can prune in early spring

Bypass pruners (shown) cut quickly and cleanly. Anvil pruners can crush stems and lead to disease.

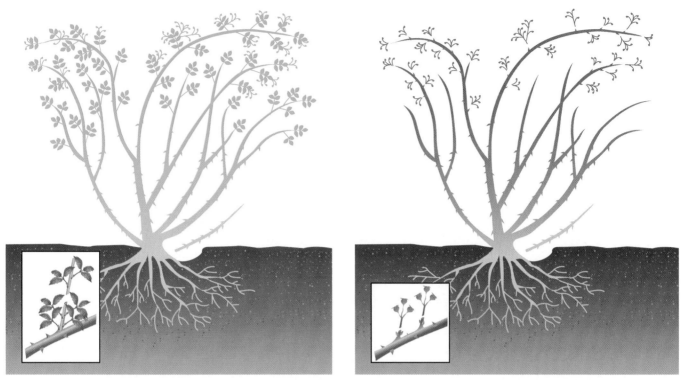

Left: On Ramblers and once-bloomers, prune after they bloom by removing old flowering canes. Keep 4 to 5 of the strongest new canes. Right: Climbing repeat-bloomers should be pruned when dormant. Remove suckers and keep the most vigorous 3 to 4 canes.

and again just before hot weather breaks in order to increase growth during the productive fall season.

The exception to the spring pruning recommendation is for roses which bloom just once each year. These roses bloom on last year's wood, and so are best pruned just after flowering. However, even with these roses, pruning to improve the plant's overall form is most easily accomplished in early spring when the bare canes expose the plant's structure. Improving the shrub's shape is often worth the sacrifice of some blossoms.

Some gardeners swear by stripping the rose bush of all its leaves a couple of weeks before spring pruning. They say that removing foliage (by cutting, never tearing it off) will trigger the development of dormant bud eyes from which stems and leaves will grow. If you try this, the location of these bud eyes will guide the

placement of your cuts. Removing foliage also helps you to see and evaluate the structure of the plant more clearly. Be sure to clean up and dispose of the leaves you remove, as these can harbor disease if left on the ground around the plant.

Equipment

Now that your plant is ready for pruning, are you properly equipped? The bare necessities are a good set of sharp hand clippers (bypass style;

A dormant rose stem with a diagonal cut above an outside bud.

not anvil) and a pair of gloves to protect your hands. An expanded tool list would include a pair of heavy-duty loppers and a pruning saw (useful if you're pruning old or overgrown rose bushes which have thick or woody stems), a pair of hedge trimmers which can speed the trimming of lots of smaller stems, and a pair of leather gloves or gauntlets which extend beyond your wrist.

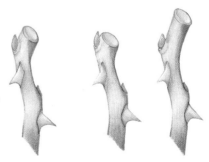

Pruning a rose stem at the right height is important. Left: Correct—about ¹/₂ inch. Center: Too short. Right: Too long. Always cut at a 45° angle with sharp bypass pruners.

A well-pruned Hybrid Tea will look like the fingers on a cupped hand, with the canes radiating from the open center.

How Much to Cut?

Depending upon the variety, condition and age of your rose, you can prune out less or more of the plant. When shortening canes, always prune back to healthy growth. Frost can often damage canes, resulting in stems which look healthy on the outside but which have damaged brown-colored pith in the center. Cut below this damage to healthy creamy-white or green pith. Light pruning involves removing canes which are old and woody, canes which are in the wrong place on the plant and canes growing in the middle of the plant which obstruct light and air. If you are happy with the overall size and shape of your rose, this is the pruning method for you. Light pruning is often suitable for cluster-flowering roses and Species roses, as it will stimulate a profusion of short-stemmed blossoms.

Moderate pruning will leave five to ten canes on the bush; the length of these remaining canes (generally from 12 inches to 48 inches) is determined by the health and variety of the rose. A good rule of thumb would be to reduce the length of these remaining canes by one-third to one-half.

Moderate pruning yields a good flush of blossoms, some of which are long-stemmed.

Severe pruning is recommended for old, weak or overgrown plants which need rejuvenation, and also for producing fewer but longer-stemmed blossoms (Hybrid Teas are charter members of this clan). After severe pruning, your plant is left with only four or five canes which are 6 inches to 18 inches tall.

Which canes to remove and which to leave? The first rule of thumb is to remove dead wood and twiggy canes by cutting them back to the nearest healthy bud eye, or if the entire cane is dead, flush with the bud union. Also remove suckers, which are growing from the rootstock rather than the grafted rose, by pruning them as close as possible to the main stem. Next remove canes which cross through the center of the plant. On full-sized rose bushes, you can also wisely remove any canes which are thinner than a pencil.

Now you can evaluate what additional cuts are needed. Consider the overall shape of the plant and its role in your garden. As you become more

CUTTINGS FROM PRUNINGS

Increase your collection of roses by rooting sections of healthy canes which you've pruned. Many roses will grow from cuttings: Rugosas, Ramblers, Old Roses, English Roses and Miniatures especially. A few, such as Hybrid Perpetuals, Albas, Damasks and Bourbons, are not successfully propagated from cuttings. Early spring trimmings aren't suitable for this purpose, but canes you cut after flowering, when the plant is in full growth, are good subjects for rooting.

In most of the country June is an ideal time. If you're going to use these trimmings, be sure to do your pruning in the morning so that the canes are full of moisture, and keep them moist, either by taking them immediately to your workbench for preparation or by wrapping the cut ends with damp paper towels and dropping them into plastic bags to retain moisture.

Cut healthy canes into sections 4 inches long, each with two to four bud eyes. Trim off lower foliage, leaving a few sets of leaves at the top of each cutting. Some rosarians recommend that you slit the exterior of the canes several times around the bottom of the cutting to encourage rooting. You may wish to insert the bottom ends into rooting hormone before potting them up in small (6 inches or so) pots filled with lightweight potting mix (seed-starting mix works well) or equal parts sand and loam. Poke a pencil into the potting mix to make holes for your cuttings, inserting several cuttings around the edge of each pot.

Stick a couple of pencils or twigs into the pot which extend above the cuttings, and drop a plastic bag over the pot to create a mini-greenhouse for your cuttings. Open up the bag each day to allow air to circulate. After 6 to 8 weeks in a brightly shaded, warm spot, the cuttings should root and send out new leaves. Remove the plastic bag, allow the cuttings to acclimate to the outside air, then pot up each cutting in its own pot. Grow them in these pots for a year before planting in the garden.

Be sure to label these cuttings with information about the parent plant so that you'll know what's what when you're ready to plant them out.

experienced in pruning your roses, you may wish to prune more severely; if you're just starting out, prune more lightly at first, for you can always cut out unwanted growth later in the season.

Bushy roses can literally be shorn with hedge clippers, a method which will yield numerous shoots and blossoms. While this method may seem overly easy, trials conducted in England have shown that roses trimmed with hedge clippers yielded the best growth in terms of plant vigor and quality of flowers. With this method, you'll still have to go in with hand clippers every few years to trim out old and dead wood, but this more time-consuming work can be limited to every few years. Roses which have a more arching growth habit will respond well to removing entire canes (cut them back flush to the graft union), thus thinning out the plant while leaving the overall arching effect of full-length canes.

Where and How to Cut

For years rosarians have recommended cutting rose canes at a 45° angle. While this is no longer considered an absolute must, it still is valuable advice as angled cuts help the exposed area shed water. Once you've decided the approximate length of the cane you wish to leave, make your cut 1/4 to 1/2 inch above the nearest outward-facing bud eye, being careful not to damage the bud eye. Pruning too close to the bud eye can damage it; making cuts too high above the bud eye will leave a stub which can become a harbor for disease and pests. Make your cuts sharp!

Do you need to seal cuts after pruning? Generally not, unless you have a problem with cane borers entering the stems through fresh wounds. Check with local rosarians or your county extension agent to see if sealing pruning wounds is recommended in your area. If so, non-toxic wood glue is an excellent sealant.

Climbers and Ramblers

Repeat-blooming Climbers should be pruned in early spring. Again, some gardeners say that they're easier to prune when stripped of their foliage. As is true with Shrub roses, Climbers need little shaping in their first few years in your garden but thereafter benefit from thinning of entire canes as well as trimming of lateral shoots. These side shoots can either be pruned back to about 3-inch lengths, leaving two to four bud eyes, or pruned more severely to leave a mere stub. The more severe pruning will produce fewer blossoms, but they will appear on sturdier stems. In thinning Climbers, leave strong-growing new canes, removing older, woody canes and thin, weak new shoots. The canes of most Climbers are productive for only a few seasons.

Ramblers are by their very definition more vigorous and require little pruning attention. In order to promote their rampant growth, thin these plants at the base. Remove up to one-third of the canes flush with the base of these once-blooming plants just after flowering each season. If they're severely overgrown, you can prune them in early spring.

Miniatures

Trim Miniature roses following the instructions for Shrub roses and you'll get much the same results. Severe pruning will produce fewer but showier blossoms; moderate to light pruning will keep the plant healthy while encouraging a good flush of blossoms.

Open up a rose bush and stimulate growth by removing dead wood and skinny canes.

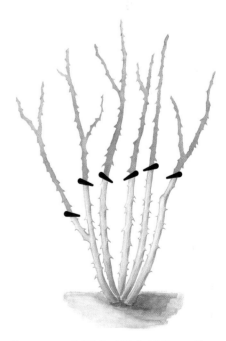

Prune an established Hybrid Tea to 3 to 5 sturdy young canes 8 to 12 inches tall. Make angled cuts 1/4 inch above outward-facing buds.

Granular fertilizer boosts a newly planted rose.

Soaker hoses keep water off foliage to protect your roses from disease.

Further Maintenance

Early spring is a good time to apply dormant oil sprays. You can apply a pre-mixed spray (be sure it is labeled for use on roses) which contains sulfur to help control fungus problems, or mix your own spray with 1 tablespoon of lightweight horticultural oil (or liquid dish soap) and 1 tablespoon of baking soda per gallon of water. Sprays which contain zinc or copper are best for preventing downy mildew.

The best thing you can do to maintain the health of your roses is to be thorough in cleaning up all the foliage and thinnings which result from your pruning. If they're diseased, it's best to throw these materials away rather than composting them.

Much Too Orderly

An old Russian proverb says "Measure nine times before you cut off once." If you extend that advice to pruning trees and shrubs, it's sound. Pruning roses isn't really that hard, but it takes a little know-how...

When I started growing roses in earnest, I learned a lot from Fred Leimkuhler, the groundskeeper of the arboretum where I worked. In Fred's Old Rose Garden, I first appreciated the virtues of 'Mme. Isaac Pereire', 'Harison's Yellow', 'Mme. Hardy', 'York and Lancaster' and many others that are now old friends.

Of all his roses, Fred's favorite was 'Maiden's Blush'. He'd hold one of the soft pink blooms in his huge hand to show me the rose's exquisite pattern and texture. We'd stand back and behold the whole bush, laden with blossoms. So when I started growing my own roses, I bought a 'Maiden's Blush' and put it right outside the kitchen window, where I could watch it mature every day. When it blooms, I thought, I'll turn my friends on to it, too.

Enter Robert, who lived downstairs. He wanted to learn about gardening in the worst way, so he volunteered to keep the yard in orderly shape. He began by just mowing and raking. Then he discovered heavy-duty weed-removal and tree-trimming equipment. He'd go off into the wild growth around the edges and clear brush and dead trees.

Early summer came on; 'Thérèse Bugnet' was blooming and 'Maiden's Blush' was growing strong and tall—full of young buds. I left town for a week in early June, looking forward to lots of new rose blooms upon my return.

When I got back home and looked out the window, all I saw was four 2-foot stubs. And there was Robert, out in the yard with lopping shears! "Robert, do you happen to know what happened to that rose bush?" I said through clenched teeth. "Oh yeah, the other day, it was drooping all over so I thought it was sick. I gave it a good pruning. Looks better, don't it?"

I am not a violent person, but I wanted to prune Robert's head clean off. Somehow, showing uncommon patience and tact, I told him that it was "drooping" because it was so heavy with buds. Its first buds ever! And in the future, please leave my rose bushes alone...and that he should ask before he cuts anything...

Well, roses are tough. My 'Maiden's Blush' recuperated, minus a year of bloom. It's done great since then and Old Fred would be proud, but I'll never forget the day it had a meeting with "Robert's Rules of Order"— in the worst way.

ROBERT WANTED TO LEARN ABOUT GARDENING IN THE WORST WAY—AND THE WORST WAY IS PRECISELY HOW IT CAME OUT.

CUTTING ROSES TO BRING INDOORS

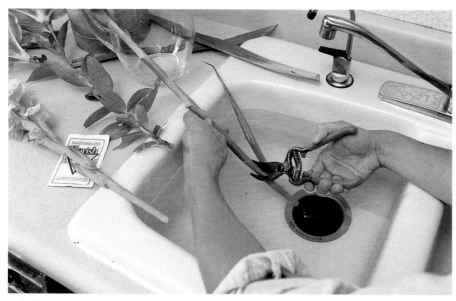

While it may seem a bit fussy, recutting the stems of cut flowers under water keeps an air bubble from forming (which blocks the transfer of water up the stem), and has a significant effect on the longevity of the flowers.

If you're like most gardeners, you can't resist bringing the garden's beauty indoors. Roses from your garden can star in a large, mixed floral arrangement. Or a single rose in a bud vase can provide a touch of simple elegance. Either way, there are a few techniques that will prolong the life and beauty of your cut roses.

As with most flowers, the best time of day to cut roses is in the evening when the air is cool and sugar reserves are high in the plant. The second best time is in the morning. Roses cut in the middle of the day often wilt and cannot be revived.

Select flowers that are just starting to open or that have opened less than half-way. By gently squeezing a flower bud in the process of opening, you can tell if a flower is close to opening. If a newly opened bud feels firm, it is not ready to pick. If the opening bud feels soft or mushy, it can be picked. The fewer petals a particular variety has, the quicker it opens, so it's best to pick single-petaled varieties at a very early stage.

When you go into the garden to cut roses, take a bucket filled with warm water and immediately plunge the flower stems in up to the bottom of the bloom. This will keep them from drying out while you cut other flowers.

Use a pair of clean, sharp pruning shears. Dull shears crush stems and do a lot of damage to plant tissue. Do not cut more than one-third of a flowering branch at a time, to avoid removing too much leaf surface and depleting the plant's ability to manufacture food. This is especially true of young rose plants. Tradition has it that you should cut the stem just above the second or third set of leaves below a flower. Make the cut at a 45° angle just above an outward-facing bud.

To keep your roses as fresh as possible, condition the flowers prior to arranging them. Remove all the foliage and thorns; foliage left under water will rot, causing bacteria build-up in the vase and significantly reducing the life of your flowers. Recut each flower, removing $1/2$ inch of stem. Cut at a sharp angle to produce as much stem surface as possible for water take-up. Then put all the freshly cut roses in a bucket with hot water (too hot for you to keep your hand in). Let the water cool, then place the entire container in the refrigerator or other cool place for 3 hours.

When you're ready to arrange your flowers, fill a clean vase with fresh, cool water. Floral preservative often helps keep bacterial growth from forming in the vase, but changing your water every day is better. Give each flower stem a fresh, angled cut under water prior to arranging.

To prolong your arrangement's vase life and keep it looking nice, place it out of bright light and hot sun. Consider moving it to a cool room or refrigerating it through the night, and again, change the water every day.

To cut a rose bloom, cut the stem just above the second or third set of leaves below a flower. Cut at a 45° angle just above an outward facing bud.

WINTER PREPARATION AND CARE

In cold areas like Zone 3, mounding winter mulch helps protect roses. A good snow cover insulates them too.

Winter hardiness varies tremendously according to rose classes and cultivars. Modern Shrub and Climbing roses generally withstand temperatures down to 10°F without winter protection (although plants with lavender, yellow, orange or bronze-colored flowers tend to be less hardy than other colors).

Hybrid Teas are generally less hardy than Floribundas.

Many Shrub and Old Garden Roses withstand winter temperatures to -10°F without protection. Rugosa roses are the hardiest of this group.

Preparing Roses for Winter

The first step in winter preparation is to plant roses appropriately hardy to your climate at the proper depth. The bud union of a grafted rose is subject to winter damage and is the point usually killed if plants are not at the correct depth or if

winter protection is not provided. (See page 105 for planting depth information.)

The second step is to have healthy, properly hardened-off plants. Roses weakened by lack of water, poor nutrition, insects or diseases will not winter well. If you garden in cold-winter climates, stop applying monthly fertilizer applications by the middle or end of July. This causes rose canes to slow their growth and allows the plant to harden off sufficiently before cold weather hits. (A mild water-soluble fertilizer can be applied to the leaves once or twice between August and September, since it supplies immediately available nutrients but does not provide long-term nutrition.)

It is also important to stop deadheading roses by August or September, depending on the length of your growing season. This allows plants to set hips and ripen. This is especially true for repeat bloomers like Hybrid Teas, which will continue to produce new shoots and blooms until a killing frost if so allowed. If you grow roses that do not form hips,

 TIP If you garden in an area where winter temperatures do not drop below 10°F (USDA Hardiness Zones 8a–11), winter protection is not necessary.

Outdoor propagation of a rose cutting.

Mound winter mulch over a bud union to protect your plant.

Mounding chopped leaves over roses before winter comes.

WINTER INJURY ON OWN-ROOT AND GRAFTED ROSES

As far as winter injury goes, own-root roses are a better bet than grafted roses, because if own-root roses are killed back to the ground, they will regrow from the rootstock fairly quickly. Grafted roses regrowing from rootstock send up watersprouts from the undesirable rootstock. Own-root Old Roses and English roses are available. Hybrid Teas are sold only as grafted plants. You can order own-root roses through mail-order sources if you can't find them at your local garden center, plus you'll have a larger selection.

simply leave the dead blooms on the plant.

Fall Preparation and Winter Protection

It isn't necessarily the absolute cold temperature that damages roses. It is often the fluctuation between intense cold and warmer temperatures. The ideal cold climate situation is to grow roses hardy to your region and for temperatures to drop gradually, then stay cold. But Mother Nature is not always cooperative, so prudent rose growers offer a steadying hand in the form of mulch. A good mulching material moderates temperature swings, reducing such freezing and thaw-

ing injuries as broken roots, split crowns and frost heaving.

There are a few steps you'll want to take in the fall prior to covering your roses. Clean up leaf debris on the ground around roses and compost it. This helps eliminate places for injurious insects and diseases to overwinter and reduces problems the following year. Remove broken canes and give your roses a final watering if the soil is not already moist.

After a couple of hard freezes have hit and night temperatures stay below freezing, it's time to cover your plants. The best form of winter protection is to mound mulching material up around the base of the canes to a height of 10 to 12 inches. The mound-

ing material should be well drained and loose.

A mixture of one-half good garden soil and one-half compost or aged manure is ideal. Do not scrape soil from around the base of the plants because roots can be injured. Get soil from another part of the garden.

Loose compost or aged sawdust will also work. Snow is an excellent insulator if you have it all winter long. Don't use

Winter protection is important for Climbers and Ramblers. Techniques include building a mound of soil or leaves for the base of a Climber and wrapping upright canes in burlap stuffed with straw.

leaves, grass clippings, straight manure or materials that would stay wet and promote disease.

After the danger of a freeze has passed and buds begin to emerge in the spring (about the same time forsythia bloom), carefully begin removing the hilling material. Remove a few inches at a time and keep some straw or mulch material handy to cover plants in case of a late frost. Do not uncover roses too soon. Considerable damage occurs if unprotected buds are breaking dormancy and a late freeze hits. Spread the hilling material over the garden as loose mulch.

Winter Protection for Climbing Roses and Standards

As mentioned before, many of the repeat-flowering Climbing roses are cold-sensitive. Most of the blooms are formed on 2- or 3-year-old wood so it is important to protect these canes in regions where winter temperatures drop below 10°F. The base of a Climber should be mounded as described previously. Additionally, canes should

be wrapped in burlap stuffed with straw.

Where temperatures drop below -10°F, remove canes from their support, bend to the ground and cover with 12 inches of soil.

In mild climates, mound roses with soil and wrap the head with straw and burlap. In colder climates, winterize roses by "tipping" and burying (see "The Minnesota Tipping Method" below for details). To save labor, grow Standards in decorative containers and move them, container and all, to an unheated garage or shed for the winter.

A WORD ABOUT ROSE CONES

Although commonly used, Styrofoam rose cones are not a good way to protect roses in the winter unless you can vent them on sunny days when heat and moisture build up inside. Additionally, rose cones often are not big enough to cover larger roses, so roses are pruned hard to fit under the cones. Many varieties should not be pruned this way and fall is rarely a good time for severe pruning.

Dormant roses mounded with wood chips for winter protection.

THE MINNESOTA TIPPING METHOD

It sounds like a new way to reward your waitress, but the Minnesota Tipping Method is really a cold-weather rose saver. In extremely cold winter areas like Zones 3 to 4 in Minnesota, "tipping" may be the only way to avoid winterkill of roses. Before temperatures reach 20°F (about October 20th), spray roses and the ground around them with a good dormant oil to reduce fungus and disease in the spring. Then tie the canes together to make them easier to handle.

Dig a trench the length of the bush. Carefully remove the soil around the base of the plant down to just below the bud union and loosen it with a spading fork. Push the bush into the

trench and cover it with 2 or 3 inches of soil.

This is more easily done by two people. One holds the canes down while the other covers the bush with soil. Cover the soil with 1½ feet of loose leaves or marsh hay. Use rodent bait to deter mice. Water the covering material and hold it in place with fencing or chicken wire. Then go have a cup of cocoa!

Around April 1st, slowly begin removing the covering material. Remove the soil gradually as it thaws. About April 15th, raise the plants to an upright position and turn on the sprinkler to keep canes wet and protected from drying winds. Work organic matter into the soil in late April.

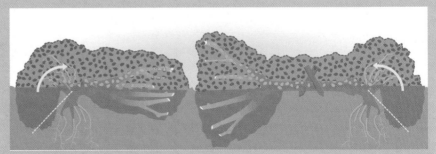

The Minnesota Tipping Method protects roses in extremely cold conditions.

PROPAGATION

If you're growing a hard-to-find rose variety, or if you happen on a wonderful old or rare rose in someone else's garden, propagating the variety yourself may be the only way to increase its numbers. Cuttings are one good way to propagate roses.

Propagation by Cuttings

Rooted cuttings are the easiest way to propagate roses, and the new plants are always true to the parent type. As mentioned previously, roses grown from cuttings (own-root roses) do not produce unwanted suckers. The disadvantage is that it takes much longer to get mature plants from cuttings than it does from roses grown by budding, and some rose varieties do not root readily. Rugosas, Ramblers, Old Roses, English roses and Miniatures usually do well from cuttings.

Softwood Cuttings

Take softwood cuttings in June from the current year's wood. Try to select wood that is between the extremes of softwood and hardwood. A good indicator of this is a stem bearing a bloom where the petals have just recently dropped off. Remove the spent bloom and take a 4-inch cutting with a bud at the top and bottom. (Hybrid Teas have fewer buds spaced farther apart than Old Roses and usually require a longer cutting.)

1. Try to get four separate sets of leaves under the bloom and a five-leaflet set at the bottom of the cutting. The reason for this is that the point at which each leaf meets the stem forms a "node" from which roots can develop.
2. Remove all leaves except for the top two sets and reduce these to two leaflets to reduce transpiration losses.
3. Dip the cutting in rooting hormone (available at most garden centers) and place in a pot with a well-drained soilless mix if you can find it. If not, use equal parts sand and loam soil. (We prefer these over standard potting mixes, which tend to stay too moist too long.) Bury the cutting to half its length.
4. Water the pot and cover with a plastic bag secured by a plastic band around the rim of the pot.
5. Check periodically to be sure that the soil doesn't dry out.
6. Place the cuttings in a warm place like a windowsill or greenhouse. They should root quickly there.
7. After roots begin to form, remove the plastic bag and transplant to another pot. Keep the pot in a protected place for 2 weeks to allow plants to become acclimated.
8. Then move the pots to a full sun area and grow until the roots are sufficiently developed to plant in the garden.
9. Congratulations! You've just propagated a new rose plant very inexpensively.

Hardwood Cuttings

The best time to take hardwood cuttings is when the canes are ripe and leaves begin to drop in the fall. Take cuttings from mature, 1-year-old wood that's at least as thick as a pencil. Cuttings should be 6 inches long with a bud at the top and bottom.

Remove leaves (if present), dust with rooting hormone, mentioned in the previous column, and place the cutting in a pot with equal parts sand and loam soil. Bury the cutting to half its length. Place the pot in a cold frame or cool greenhouse. In milder winter climates, an alternative to planting in pots is to plant hardwood cuttings in a sheltered, warm part of the garden with well-drained soil.

Either way, hardwood cuttings should start to root by early spring and grow into small bushes by early autumn when they can be transplanted to their permanent home.

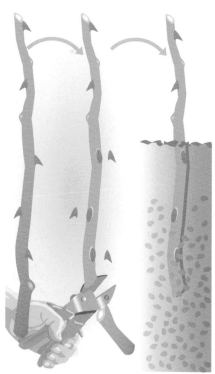

Hardwood cuttings should be from 1-year-old wood; at least pencil-thick; and 6 inches long with a bud at the top and bottom. Bury the cutting to half its length until it has rooted and is large enough to transplant.

« CHAPTER 6 »

DISEASES AND PESTS

Once you've selected vigorous roses well suited to your climate and planted them with care, you've made a good start toward growing healthy plants. Yet fungal diseases and insect pests are likely to find your roses eventually, and thoughtful intervention will be needed. Depending on the severity of the problem, your response may be to promptly prune away infected plant parts or to even completely replace a particularly weak plant.

In this chapter, you'll gain the knowledge needed to make smart decisions when your roses are faced with challenges from any of a dozen well-known pests and pathogens.

Throughout this book, we've emphasized selecting strong, trouble-tolerant roses, and growing them in ways that are satisfying for both the gardener and the plants. Things are no different when pests are in the spotlight, for no gardener should ever feel obligated to risk their health or principles for the sake of a flower. By practicing preventive health care with your roses, you can enjoy fragrant blooms without feeling chained to a sprayer.

In this book, we are committed to sound ecological practices, and we strongly recommend the following:

1. Try the most benign treatment first. If it doesn't work, move to the next least harmful measure. Don't immediately break out the harsh chemicals when you have a pest or disease problem.
2. Don't use broad-spectrum insecticides. They kill beneficial insects and upset your garden's ecological balance.
3. Choose the most specific treatment for the problem. *Always* read the label and follow directions.

ROSES AS HOST PLANTS

Knocking Japanese beetles into a jar of soapy water is a benign way to control insect pests. Pay kids a penny per beetle and make them Rose Rangers!

With very few exceptions, the insects and diseases that injure roses have a very narrow range of acceptable host plants. One of the best known diseases of the rose, black spot, is often called rose black spot since the fungus that causes the disease is unable to infect plants other than roses.

Preventive sprays, applied at the right time, can be effective.

This is important to remember if your garden includes many different types of plants, for it is easy to erroneously assume that the powdery mildew on your phlox or the early blight on your tomatoes can spread to infect your roses. Certainly the environmental conditions that contribute to disease problems with other plants also can lead to trouble for roses, but plant diseases—and most insects—usually require the presence of very specific plants. In the case of most rose pests, those host plants can only be roses.

The Geographical Factor

Just as climate affects the growth habits, leaf color and sometimes bloom patterns of roses, it also influences their risk of developing problems with pests. In the eastern United States, for example, you can count on having to do battle with Japanese beetles, which are less well known in the West and Midwest (although they do sometimes crop up in places). Damp climates contribute to problems with black spot and aphids, while arid conditions may aggravate your efforts to control spider mites and pow-

TIP — **KEEPING RECORDS**

If you are new to growing roses, or have recently added a number of new roses to your garden, one of the most important tools for managing pest problems is keeping records of your own observations. Use a notebook or index cards to write down when you see pests or diseases on specific cultivars, along with what measures you took to control the problem. Since diseases in particular are easier to prevent than to cure, this information will be enormously helpful in future seasons, and may help reduce the amount of intervention needed to keep persistent problems at bay. Your records also will show patterns of infection that might be related to site problems, such as not enough air circulation or sunshine.

dery mildew. As you learn more about how your climate affects the health of your roses, use that knowledge to choose cultivars that are best able to stand up to locally prevalent pests.

Whether it's Milky Spore or any other chemical treatment, always read the label and follow instructions for your own safety and for your plants' health.

PREVENTIVE CARE FOR HEALTHY ROSES

- Plant roses where they will get copious fresh air and full morning sun.
- Prune off diseased leaves and twigs as soon as you see them.
- Pick up fallen leaves and flowers promptly.
- Mulch! And replace mulch material at least once a year (see pp. 112-113).

- Use drip irrigation, or water so that rose foliage has a chance to dry before nightfall.
- Fertilize regularly to support strong growth.
- Isolate plants that appear susceptible to diseases.
- Control insect populations early.
- Diversify your collection to include different types of roses.

Japanese beetle traps are so effective that they may attract the pests to your garden. It's better to place them downwind from your roses.

SPRAY SAFELY

- Always try the least toxic method of pest control first.
- When using fungicides or insecticides on your roses, always read and follow label instructions exactly.
- Use only chemicals specifically labeled for use on roses. Never use any product on a plant not listed on its label.
- Mix only as much spray solution as you will use that day.

- Use spray equipment that you can comfortably handle.
- Dress appropriately to protect your skin, nose and eyes from contact with chemicals.
- Wear a mask when handling any type of dust.
- Never use a sprayer that has been used to apply herbicides (weed killers).
- Never spray when windy conditions can cause drift.

Earth-Safe Intervention

The tremendous popularity of—some would say fixation on—Hybrid Tea roses during the past few decades has made many gardeners believe that they have to adhere strictly to an ongoing spray program to grow roses. There is certainly some basis in truth here, for growing show-quality Hybrid Teas in many climates does indeed require that plants receive constant protection from fungal diseases and insects.

However, thanks to the work of rose conservationists, modern rose breeders and the acceptance of the standard we'll call "garden-quality roses," it's certainly possible for most gardeners to grow many roses without using chemical pesticides. In the final analysis, each gardener must make a personal decision on the issue of pesticides by balancing practical and ethical considerations. Throughout this chapter, we will provide both natural and chemical solutions to rose pest problems, again suggesting that you try the lowest-impact methods first.

LOW-IMPACT PESTICIDES

The following types of products are less toxic than many widely used pesticides, and should be your first line of defense against rose problems.

Substance	What It Does	Safety
Light Horticultural Oil	Thinly coats rose leaves with oil, which strengthens their resistance to such fungi as black spot and powdery mildew. Also discourages aphids, scale and other small insects.	Poses no risk to humans. But when used in temperatures above 90°F, rose leaves may be damaged.
Insecticidal Soap	Kills aphids and spider mites. Decreases feeding by slugs. May aid in preventing foliar diseases caused by fungi.	Poses no risk to humans. But when used on hot, dry days, rose leaves may be damaged.
Lime-sulfur Spray	Applied when roses are fully dormant in winter, it kills powdery mildew, scale and other pests that overwinter on rose stems.	Naturally derived yet highly caustic. Follow all safety precautions described on label. Apply only to *dormant* plants, as this substance can seriously damage leaves.
Neem	Radically reduces insect feeding until insects die. Appropriate for control of Japanese beetles and other insects that consume rose leaves and flowers.	Naturally derived. Since neem does not kill insects on contact, it usually causes no harm to beneficial insects—only insects that are actively feeding on treated plants.
Beneficial Nematodes	Applied to soil in summer, nematodes kill pupae of rose midge, rose sawfly (slug) and many other pests.	Naturally occurring and safe for humans. Not effective unless applied in warm weather when pests are present in the soil.

MAJOR ROSE DISEASES

Clip off foliage infected with black spot and dispose of it. Don't put it in compost; it may spread.

sands of new spores. Fungal spores live from year to year on stems, fallen leaves, mulch, wild roses and brambles. Because the spores are so tiny, numerous and easily spread about, it is not realistic to think you can keep them out of your rose garden at all times. Instead, get to know each type of fungus and how it grows, along with ways to protect your roses from infection.

Some symptoms that look like diseases are actually physiological disorders which develop when roses cannot take up certain nutrients, or are subjected to stressful weather. Several such disorders are described in detail on page 135.

Rose Black Spot

The most prevalent disease of roses, rose black spot is caused by a fungus. The fungus establishes itself on rose leaves that are damp for more than 6 hours at a time, and when nighttime temperatures are between 59°F and 80°F.

Dark circular spots with fringed edges develop on either side of the leaves. As the spots enlarge, they are often surrounded by a yellow halo. When the spots become numerous, infected leaves turn yellow and drop off. A severely infected plant can be completely defoliated by black spot, leading to its quick demise. Hybrid Teas and some types of Old Roses are most susceptible. Shrub and landscape roses offer varying levels of resistance.

Intervention

When you see a small outbreak of black spot on a resistant rose, clip off the infected

Most rose diseases are caused by fungi, which are microscopic life forms that closely resemble tiny parasitic plants. These fungi live on rose leaves, stems and sometimes flowers. They become established when spores blow on the wind or spread in droplets of windblown rain, landing on rose leaves. The spores germinate, then develop rootlike organs called haustoria that penetrate into leaves and speed toward maturity at which time they release hundreds or thou-

Black spot is an ugly fungal disease that strikes in damp conditions.

foliage right away. Also pick up any leaves that may have fallen to the ground on their own. Check nearby twigs for dark circular spots and prune them off if necessary.

To manage black spot on susceptible roses, make a mixture of 2 tablespoons light horticultural oil and 1 gallon water, and thoroughly apply it to your plants once a week during periods of rainy weather. Do not use oil when daytime temperatures are above 90°F, as it can cause injury to plant leaves. You also may use a properly labeled fungicide to prevent black spot, or alternate applications of horticultural oil with applications of fungicide. This approach gives good control while reducing the frequency of fungicide applications by half.

RESISTANT ROSES

Any rose can become infected with black spot, but Rugosa and Shrub roses are somewhat resistant. When tough Old Roses become infected, they often recover and regain their strength the following season. Tall Climbers tend to hold their foliage so high that it dries quickly, making them less susceptible to this disease. Resistance varies widely among Hybrid Teas. For example, 'Cary Grant' is often tolerant, while 'Peace' is generally susceptible.

THE LANGUAGE OF RESISTANCE

Whether or not a certain rose will fall victim to a specific disease is strongly affected by its genetic makeup. Four words are used to describe the degree to which different cultivars may be parasitized by disease-causing fungi:

- *Susceptible* means that the rose in question is easy prey to a certain fungus. If the spores are present and conditions are favorable, a susceptible rose will almost certainly get the disease.
- *Tolerant* means the rose may become infected rather easily, yet has some ability to defend itself, either by growing new leaves or staying alive despite being seriously infected.
- *Resistant* means the rose is very slow to get the disease, at least when compared to other cultivars, and usually recovers when slightly infected.
- *Immune* is never used when discussing rose diseases, for no roses are truly immune to any fungus that infects plants of the rose family.

Preventive Care

Start with good soil and use compost (see Chapter 5 for best growing techniques). Prune and fertilize roses as needed to support vigorous growth. Each year, lay down a fresh layer of a spongy organic mulch such as pine needles, shredded pine bark or oat straw. These types of mulches reduce splashing of spores and may trap spores that are washed to the ground. Replenish your mulch as needed to keep soil covered well.

Keep the foliage as dry as possible at all times. Never water in the evening so that rose leaves will remain wet overnight. Better yet, install and use a drip irrigation system. It waters roots better, eliminates wasteful evaporation and doesn't wet your foliage. It will probably cut your water bill too!

Powdery Mildew

This rose disease, caused by fungus, is most prevalent on the West Coast, but small outbreaks can occur anywhere on a wide variety of roses. The first symptoms develop on tender young leaves in mid to late spring, when temperatures range between 60° and 70°F. Affected leaves appear pale and limp, with curled edges. Within a few days, white powdery deposits are clearly visible on leaves, stems and young buds. If conditions are favorable, all of the

Powdery mildew is another fungal condition that sometimes hits roses.

new growth on nearby parts of the plant become infected.

Intervention

Immediately clip off affected plant parts and dispose of them. Older leaves that have turned dark green seldom become infected, but tender stems and new buds close to the site of the initial infection often host spores. Spray plants thoroughly with a strong stream of water to dislodge spores that have not yet established themselves on leaves. (But again, don't leave foliage wet at night.)

Preventive Care

Where powdery mildew is a continuing problem, be sure to clean up all fallen leaves at the end of the season, and replace mulch material every spring. Prune plants to facilitate good air circulation and remove clearly susceptible plants from the garden. If you cannot bear to part with them, try growing them in containers placed in a well-ventilated spot. As soon as temperatures rise into the 60s in spring, spray your roses weekly with a mixture of 3 teaspoons baking soda and 2 tablespoons light horticultural oil per gallon of water. Be very careful when using horticultural oil on roses in hot weather (above 90° F), as it may cause injury to the leaves. Thoroughly spraying plants with water between applications of an oil mixture helps wash off some of the oil, thus reducing this risk. If powdery mildew problems develop despite these measures, treat plants with an appropriately labeled fungicide every 7 to 10 days.

In winter, spray plants with lime-sulfur to eliminate overwintering spores. Since tender new growth is at high risk for powdery mildew, withholding applications of high nitrogen fertilizer in midspring can be helpful in managing this disease.

Rose Rust

Rose rust is most common in foggy, cool areas near the Pacific Coast. Summer temperatures above 80°F keep it suppressed elsewhere, especially where there is little natural rainfall. Like black spot, rust spores require wet leaves to germinate and grow. Rust spots are small clusters of cinnamon-like powder, and they usually develop on the undersides of leaves. On the tops of infected leaves, yellow patches may appear. When the disease is quite advanced, the brownish deposits may be found all over leaves and stems. In fall, the color of the fungal spores changes from reddish brown to black.

If you have seen rust on your roses before, make a habit of checking leaf undersides every two weeks, beginning in midspring. If you can catch this disease early, pruning off infected plant parts will often stop its progress. Sulfur-based fungicides are usually effective in controlling rust. The same cultural techniques that help prevent black spot (page 129) will have a huge impact on future problems with rust.

Rose rust on a stem.

RESISTANT ROSES

Roses with shiny, leathery leaves (for example, the Meidilands) have few problems with powdery mildew. Many other roses show very limited infection. Don't be alarmed if a plant shows only a few infected leaves in spring or fall, when cool weather prevails. At the same time, keep notes of the roses in your garden that repeatedly become infected, as well as their location. Sites that limit sunshine and air circulation may be best planted with flowers other than roses.

Virus

Occasionally you may notice that one of your plants appears to have leaves lightly variegated with yellow spots or small streaks. Rather than being an ornamental feature, this is evidence that the plant is infected with rose virus. Sometimes infected plants will prosper and bloom reasonably well, but more often they are weak growers that produce misshapen buds and flowers. Over time, infected plants appear stunted and lack vigor compared to normal ones.

Virus is typically transmitted when plants are grafted at the nursery, and does not spread among plants in the garden. It is very rare on plants that are grown on their own roots. Replace obviously infected plants with healthy ones. When grafting your own roses, clean your tools in a weak bleach solution as a precaution against the possible spread of this or other diseases.

Downy Mildew

This disease is rare in home gardens where roses receive regular care. However, very high humidity, cool temperatures and seriously crowded foliage can create the dank conditions required for this devastating fungus. On rose leaves, downy mildew appears as dark scorched patches on leaves, which quickly run together until the leaves wither. It is best prevented with cultural techniques including regular pruning and exposure of all leaves to fresh air and sunshine. Should this disease appear on roses in the fall, treat your plants with a sulfur-based fungicide when they become dormant in the winter.

Gall Infection

Hybrid Teas and some other roses are created by grafting cuttings onto a rootstock that gives the plants improved cold-

Gall infection on a Hybrid Tea.

hardiness and vigor. Grafted plants show an enlarged lump of woody tissue just above the soil line, called the graft union. Occasionally this graft union becomes infected with a bacterium that causes the graft union to show rough, rounded growths, or galls, on the surface of the graft union. Galls sometimes develop on the low sections of the stem and uppermost roots, too. Infected roses grow slowly, if at all, and do not flower well.

This disease usually can be traced to the nursery, for it is usually spread by using contaminated instruments or plant material during the grafting process. Rough hoeing or cultivating around plants, so that the base of the plant is accidentally nicked, also can give rise to this infection. To be on the safe side, remove any gall-infected rose from the garden, and replace it with a healthy plant.

Nematodes

Nematodes are microscopic worms that live in the soil. Several species become parasites of plants when they enter the roots and reproduce within root tissues. The most destructive species, called rootknot nema-

todes, cause host plants to develop knotty bumps on their roots. These knots impair the plant's ability to take up water and soil-borne nutrients, so it always appears thirsty and malnourished. Rootknot nematodes are quite common in sandy soils in warm climates. They cannot survive in the cold soils of the north.

If your soil is sandy and you live in Zones 8, 9 or 10, have your soil tested for the presence of rootknot nematodes, or contact your local extension service to find out if rootknot nematodes are common in your area. If they do pose a risk, shop for roses locally that have been grafted onto *Rosa fortuniana* rootstocks. Sometimes called "Florida roses," this rootstock gives roses a high level of resistance to nematodes, and also helps roses flourish in sandy soil. In addition to this rootstock, some Old Roses that grow on their own roots show good natural resistance to nematodes, including China Roses and Ramblers. Routine enrichment of the soil with organic matter prior to planting roses also goes a long way toward preventing nematode problems, and is a good gardening practice anywhere.

INSECT PESTS OF ROSES

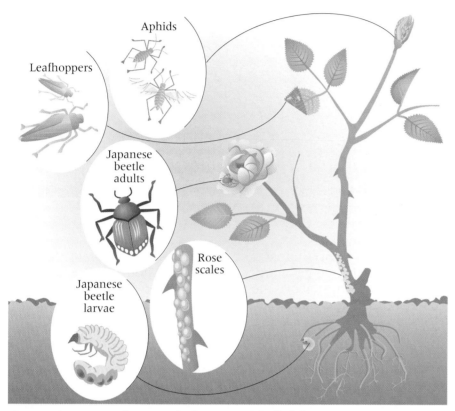

Common insect pests of roses, and where you might find them.

Aphids suck out plant juices when natural predators (ladybugs, lacewings) aren't around to control them. Aphids are easily handled by a blast of water or a spray of insecticidal soap.

If you learn to identify the insects that damage roses, you've taken the best step toward controlling them. Insects vary from region to region, and in some regions roses have few insect pests. When insects do appear on roses, early intervention can be critical. Simply removing the insects from the plants often keeps damage at tolerable levels. All roses can withstand slight insect feeding, yet become weakened when insects damage more than about 30 percent of the plant's leaves.

Use the information in these pages to help you identify rose pests and learn more about their life cycles. Most destructive insects start out as eggs, then become larvae and after feeding, grow or pupate into adults. Depending on the species, control is usually most effective when targeted toward a specific stage of an insect's development.

Aphids

These small insects usually feed in groups on tender young stems and buds, and are most often seen in spring and early summer. They are typically $1/8$ inch long, and may be brown, green or reddish in color. Aphids sink their sharp mouthparts into plant tissues and suck out plant juices. In this way, they weaken the stems and slow the emergence of new growth.

Numerous natural predators attack aphids, including lady beetles (ladybugs) and lacewing larvae. You can easily interrupt aphid feeding by spraying infested plant parts weekly with a strong spray of water. If a plant is heavily infested and no predator activity is apparent, use insecticidal soap to bring the problem under control.

Leafcutter Bees

Although generally considered beneficial insects, leafcutter bees damage roses by cutting out circular sections of leaf, which they use to build their nests. You may never see the dark, shiny $1/2$-inch-long-bees, but the symmetrical semicircles cut from the leaves are unmistakable evidence of leafcutter bee activity. The damage is usually light, and easily tolerated by healthy plants. No control is recommended.

Japanese Beetles

Japanese beetles are formidable rose pests in the Northeast, the Mid-Atlantic region and much of the upper South. In early summer, the copper-colored adult beetles emerge in large numbers and feed intensively for about six weeks. During spring

Japanese beetles cluster on a rose bud. Get out the jar of soapy water!

and fall, the larvae are white grub worms, which feed on grass roots just beneath the soil. Adult Japanese beetles damage a number of different plants, but roses are probably their favorites. When the beetles are at their peak, it's not unusual to find several feeding in a single blossom. They also eat rose leaves.

There are several ways to reduce Japanese beetle problems, but since the beetles are so mobile it is helpful if your neighbors also become involved. Beware of Japanese beetle traps, which do attract and kill thousands of beetles, but may also attract this pest to your yard! If you use traps, place them 400 feet downwind of your roses.

Here are the most effective control measures:

1. Apply Milky Spore disease to lawn areas. This naturally occurring bacterium infects Japanese beetle larvae and gradually reduces the local population. It is most effective 2 years after application and may last up to 20 years. (It will help your lawn too.)
2. Apply beneficial nematodes to the soil when the soil temperature is above 55°F and the larvae are close to the surface. During this window of opportunity, you also may apply a low-toxicity pesticide to the soil. The insecticide known as Merit is much less toxic to mammals, birds and fish than other soil insecticides. Look on the label of products intended for use against white grubs to find the word Merit, or look for "imidacloprid" listed as the main active ingredient.
3. Hand-pick adult beetles from rose plants. Knock them into a jar of soapy water to kill them.
4. Apply a neem-based insecticide to rose plants when the beetles are too numerous to remove by hand.

Rose Midges

When young leaf tips and green buds suddenly wilt and blacken, you are probably seeing damage caused by the rose midge. This tiny brown fly, native to North America, lays eggs on tender young growth. The eggs hatch, then maggots burrow inside the stem and girdle it from the inside out as they feed. Cut off affected stems, and apply beneficial nematodes to the soil below infested plants to kill the pupae, thus preventing a second generation.

Spider Mites

These microscopic members of the spider family are often the cause of leaves that suddenly appear bleached with hundreds of tiny yellow-brown specks in midsummer. Spider mites are always most active in hot, dry weather. They feed on leaf undersides in large numbers, sucking out plant juices. The mites themselves are too small to see, but you may be able to see a faint white webbing on the undersides of badly infested leaves.

To prevent spider mite problems or bring light infestations under control, thoroughly wash leaf undersides with clear water every two weeks beginning in early summer. Use a spray wand to make sure you get a strong spray of water capable of dislodging these tiny creatures. Treat established infestations with insecticidal soap three times at 5-day intervals. Damaged leaves will not regain their color when the spider mites are gone, but you should see no evidence of their presence on new leaves.

Scales

These tiny $^1/_{10}$-inch-long insects cling to rose stems and canes, and suck out plant juices. Their backs are covered with oval gray or brown shells. As you watch them, they do not appear to move. You can gently scrape off widely scattered scale with a fingernail, or simply prune out badly infested canes. Spraying dormant plants with lime-sulfur in winter eliminates any over-

Red spider mite damage.

BENEFICIAL INSECTS

You'll often see insects on your roses that do not damage the plants. In many cases these are predatory insects that can be your most valuable allies in controlling problem pests. One of the main reasons not to use broad-spectrum insecticides (which kill all types of insects) is to safeguard your garden's population of beneficial creatures. Numerous species of flies, wasps, beetles and other insects make up a garden's beneficial community. Growing plants that produce small flowers near your roses helps provide many beneficial insects with habitat and food.

Rose weevils can damage blooms. Pick them off as you would beetles.

wintering individuals. During the summer, light horticultural oil or insecticidal soap will bring serious scale problems under control.

Rose Slugs

Three species of rose slug may occur on roses in North America, especially in cool climates. These small green worms, which grow up to ⁵/₈ of an inch long, feed on rose leaves by rasping away the green tissue until the leaves have a skeletonized appearance, consisting only of veins and thin tan patches. Rose slugs are the larvae of small, shiny black and yellow wasps called sawflies. The adults are seldom seen in the garden. After laying their eggs, they promptly fly away.

Pick off rose slugs when you see them, and drown them in a jar of soapy water. If the slugs are too numerous to hand pick, use a neem-based insecticide to bring them under control.

Thrips

So small and hidden that they are almost impossible to see, thrips lurk inside unopened flower buds and the stems below. This pest is most commonly seen in white and light-colored roses. Infested buds droop sideways and may fail to open. If they do open, petals show unusual brown speckles, streaks and bumps. If you shake such a

Milky Spore thwarts flower scarab beetles.

blossom over a piece of black paper, you may be able to see the yellowish sliver-sized thrips.

Thrips can complete their life cycle by the time a rose blossom falls apart, at which time the adults fly on primitive wings to start a new generation on new rose buds. Removing infested blossoms from the garden interrupts this process, as does deadheading roses that may have some thrips inside, though no damage is apparent. Since thrips have numerous natural predators and feed inside buds where sprays cannot touch them, tolerance and cleanup of old blossoms are the best controls. Where problems are continuous, emphasize dark-colored roses in your garden rather than light ones.

Rose chafer beetles deserve the soapy water treatment too.

ANIMAL PESTS

Rose thorns deter many animals, but when food is scarce it is possible to lose roses to hungry rabbits or deer. Sturdy fences are the best defense, and may be the only way to protect plants in areas where animal pressure is very severe. For rabbits, a wire mesh fence that reaches 6 inches below ground and 2 feet high is sufficient. Or you can surround each plant with a chicken wire cage.

Since deer are terrific jumpers, fencing them out may require an 8-foot-high fence made of wood, chicken wire or polyester net-

ting. Deer won't jump into a spot they can't see, so a 4 to 5-foot fence, with closely planted evergreens inside it, will often work. Some people have good results with a 3-strand electric fence too. Where fencing is not practical, surround roses with aromatic herbs to help discourage deer feeding. Dogs kept outdoors at night may keep deer out of your rose garden too, though you will have to endure their barking.

Rodents that burrow underground, including moles, voles and gophers, sometimes damage rose roots. Treating mole tunnels

with a mixture of castor oil and soap (commercially sold as Mole-Med) is surprisingly effective. Voles often follow in the abandoned tunnels of moles, and occasionally chew on canes of roses. If you have no cat to chase them away, capture voles in mousetraps placed around plants at night.

Where gophers are a serious problem, it is best to grow roses in roomy containers sunk down into the ground. Large, long-lived Climbers may be planted in large chicken wire baskets to protect their roots from gopher damage.

PHYSIOLOGICAL DISORDERS

The following symptoms may look like they have been caused by an insect or disease, but they are really physiological disorders that develop in response to weather, fertility or cultural factors.

Funny Bud

When a period of warm spring weather (encouraging fast growth of new stems, leaves and buds) is followed by several cold days, the new buds may grow very little and bend over at odd angles. This disorder is called funny bud, but it's not funny when your roses get it. Affected flowers will not develop properly, and are best snipped off. The flowers that form later, when warm weather returns, should be normal.

Iron Chlorosis

When roses grow in alkaline soils with a high pH, the iron in the soil may not be available to plants. When this happens, young leaves turn yellowish between the green leaf veins, and older leaves may show some yellowing as well. Adjusting the soil to make it slightly more acidic, either by working in a light dusting of sulfur or by digging acidic soil amendments into the soil, should solve the problem. You can spray badly affected plants with an iron supplement. (Remember, roses like a slightly acidic soil—6.5 to 6.8 pH. Test your soil regularly.)

Graft Failure

When a rose produces flowers that do not have the color or form of the cultivar that you initially planted, and you can see stems arising directly from the soil, it is likely that you planted a grafted rose and the grafted part (above the lumpy graft union at the base of the main stem) has died. The new flower-producing stems are those from the root stock, which is usually a vigorous

Mosaic virus is a pervasive disease of roses that is spread by infected rootstock. Buy certified virus-free stock whenever possible.

Species Rose rather than a showy Hybrid Tea or Floribunda. If you do not care for the rose, dig it up and replace it with a new plant. Plant the culprit elsewhere or give it to a neighbor.

Herbicide Drift

If the leaves of a rose become thin and stringy, and the plant does not grow well and hardly flowers at all, the plant may have been exposed to an herbicide used to control nearby weeds. If the damage occurs late in the season and the plant is otherwise healthy, keep it for another year. The new foliage produced the following spring will probably be normal. If the symptoms return, replace the plant.

Iron chlorosis happens when iron is "locked up" by the soil's high pH. Lower the pH to counteract this condition.

❦ CHAPTER 7 ❧

SIMPLY THE BEST

RESOURCES FOR ROSE GROWING

In this chapter, we've compiled a big list of the best roses for specific gardening purposes. By now you know that roses serve several purposes in the garden. We use "only" 17 categories, and could expand that list if space permitted.

For almost a year we've combed the rose world for suggestions. We asked all of the contributors to this book and all our rose gardening friends for their recommendations. (Collectively we've got well over a century of gardening experience.) We've also consulted professional organizations, other rose books and years' worth of magazine articles written by people expert in the art of rose gardening.

You'll also find a glossary packed with terms from the world of roses, to add to your knowledge base and serve as a reference resource.

THE BEST ROSES: TRY THESE FOR SUCCESS

One of the best roses for shadier conditions: 'Félicité Parmentier'.

For fragrance: Rosa centifolia.

For shadier conditions: 'Königin von Dänemark'.

Shade-Tolerant
'Félicité Parmentier'
'Königin von
    Dänemark'
'Ballerina'
'Great Maiden's Blush'
'Mme. Hardy'
'Rose de Rescht'
'Christian Dior'

'Garden Party'
'Fred Edmunds'
'Nymphenburg'
'Erfurt'

For Fragrance
Rosa centifolia
'Chrysler Imperial'
'Double Delight'
'Louise Odier'
'Mme. Hardy'
'Mme. Isaac Pereire'
'Communis'
'Blanc Double de
    Coubert'
'Fragrant Cloud'
'Fragrant
    Memory'
'Tiffany'

For fragrance: 'Double Delight'.

'Ballerina' will dance when the lights are low.

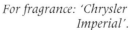

For fragrance: 'Chrysler Imperial'.

Climbers and Ramblers: 'Dortmund'.

For Landscaping
'The Fairy'
'Celsiana'
'Ballerina'
'Carefree Wonder'
'Nearly Wild'
'Henry Hudson'
'Blanc Double de
   Coubert'
'Dainty Bess'
'Graham Thomas'
'Scarlet Meidiland'
'Pink Meidiland'

For continuous blooming habit: 'Iceberg'.

For Continuous Bloom
'Iceberg' (not for
   Zone 5)
'Bonica'
'The Fairy'
'John Davis'
'Charles Albanel'
'Frau Dagmar Hartopp'
'Jens Munk'
'Schneezwerg'
'Parkdirektor Riggers'
'Stanwell Perpetual'

For landscape uses: 'The Fairy'.

'Iceberg', grown here with bougainvillea, can bloom season-long.

Climbers/ Ramblers
'Cécile Brunner'
'Dortmund'
'Champney's Pink
   Cluster'

'John Cabot'
'Sally Holmes'
'Max Graf'
'New Dawn'
'William Baffin'

For landscape uses: 'Celsiana'.

Climbers and Ramblers: 'Climbing Cécile Brunner'.

Climbers and Ramblers: 'Champney's Pink Cluster'.

'The Fairy' in a landscape setting.

*For continous bloom:
'Bonica'.*

For Repeat Bloom
'Blanc Double de
    Coubert'
'Hansa'
'Nearly Wild'
'Betty Prior'
'Rose de Rescht'

For large blooms, give 'Peace' a chance.

'Dortmund'
'Carefree
    Beauty'
'Morden
    Centennial'
'Moje
    Hammarberg'
'Nevada'

For Large Blooms
'Peace'
'Dolly Parton'

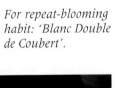

*For repeat-blooming
habit: 'Blanc Double
de Coubert'.*

For repeat bloom: 'Hansa'.

*For large blooms: 'Dolly
Parton'.*

For repeat bloom: 'Nearly Wild'.

For Cutting

'Mme. Isaac Pereire'
'Louise Odier'
Rosa banksiae lutea
'Mr. Lincoln'
'Iceberg'
'Peace'
'Touch of Class'
'Champney's Pink
  Cluster'
'Mermaid'
'Sombreuil'

One of the best for cutting: 'Louise Odier'.

'Mister Lincoln' provides exquisite cuttings.

For Disease Resistance

'Graham Thomas'
'Stanwell Perpetual'
'Carefree Wonder'
'Max Graf'
'Scarlet Meidiland'
'Bonica'
'Bredon'
'Dortmund'
'William Baffin'
'Königin von
  Dänemark'

For disease resistance, 'Carefree Wonder' lives up to its name.

For a fragrant cutting: 'Mme. Isaac Pereire'.

For abundant cuttings, it's hard to top "Yellow Lady Banks' Rose," R. banksiae lutea.

'Stanwell Perpetual' is highly resistant to disease.

For a disease-resistant rose, grow 'Graham Thomas'.

For Rose Hips/ Habitat

'Ballerina'
'Frau Dagmar Hartopp'
Rosa rugosa alba
'Scabrosa'
'Alba Semi-plena'
'Nastarana'
Rosa eglanteria

For abundant rose hips, try 'Ballerina'.

Rose hips provide winter interest and feed the birds too.

Thornless

'Zéphirine Drouhin'
'Marie Pavié'
Rosa banksiae banksiae
'Paul Neyron'
Rosa palustris

'Zéphirine Drouhin' is as thornless as they come.

'Queen Elizabeth' remains cool and collected when the heat is on.

'Thérèse Bugnet', bred in Canada, shrugs off the cold.

Cold-Tolerant

'Thérèse Bugnet'
'Alba Semi-plena'
'Betty Bland'
'Henry Kelsey'
Rosa rugosa
'Rose des Peintres'
'John Davis'
'Prairie Youth'
'William Baffin'

Heat-Tolerant

'Queen Elizabeth'
'Heritage'
'Othello'
Rosa chinensis varieties
'Iceberg'
Rosa laevigata
'Mevrouw Nathalie
   Nypels'

Cold-hardy roses include Prof. Buck's "Prairie" series. Here, 'Prairie Wren'.

The English roses 'Heritage' (left) and 'Othello' tolerate warm conditions.

'Altissimo' will take wet conditions.

Tolerant of Wet Conditions

'Altissimo'
'Constance Spry'
'Sally Holmes'
'Thérèse Bugnet'
'Dortmund'

'Constance Spry' stays lively even when it's wet out.

'Touch of Class' stays cool in hot and dry conditions.

For winter interest: 'Nastarana'.

Close-up of 'Betty Prior'.

As Hedges
'Betty Prior'
'Heritage'
'Abbotswood'
Rosa eglanteria
'Scabrosa'
'Frau Dagmar Hartopp'

Rosa sericea var. *pteracantha*

For dry conditions: R. banksiae lutea *("Yellow Lady Banks' Rose")*

'Old Blush' can jazz up gardens in the South.

'Betty Prior' makes a fine hedge.

Tolerant of Dry Conditions
'Touch of Class'
'Souvenir de la
   Malmaison'
Rosa banksiae lutea
Rosa laevigata
'Mermaid'
'Old Blush'

For Winter Interest
'Old Blush'
'Nastarana'
'Martin Frobisher'

'Souvenir de la Malmaison' will tolerate dry times.

English roses are excellent hedge choices: 'Heritage'.

HOT DIXIELAND CHOICES

Here's Alabama gardener Barbara Pleasant's list of the best roses for the South's long, hot, steamy summers and mild winters:

Shrub and Landscaping Roses

'Carefree Wonder'
'Graham Thomas'
'Heritage'
Rosa rugosa varieties
'The Fairy'

Climbing Roses

'Altissimo'
'America'
'Golden Showers'
Rosa banksiae banksiae
'New Dawn'

Floribundas

'Betty Prior'

'Europeana'
'Iceberg'

Grandifloras

'Gold Medal'
'Queen Elizabeth'

Hybrid Teas

'Double Delight'
'Mister Lincoln'
'Touch of Class'

Old and Species Roses

Rosa chinensis mutabilis
'Cécile Brunner'
'Félicité Parmentier'
'Old Blush'

SOURCES

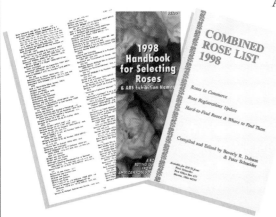

General Information on Roses

National Home Gardening Club Web Site

http://www.gardeningclub.com

Turn to our Web site for all kinds of gardening information, including rose updates.

Combined Rose List

If you want to know which company offers a particular rose, get a copy of the rose grower's source bible, the *Combined Rose List*. The CRL tells you where to buy hard-to-find roses from both North American and overseas nursery sources. It includes rose registrations and correct classifications too.

The *Combined Rose List* is updated regularly. You can purchase a copy for $19.50 postpaid ($21.00 for 1st-class mail delivery) from Peter Schneider, P.O. Box 677, Mantua, OH 44255.

ARS Handbook for Selecting Roses

Each year, the American Rose Society (ARS) publishes an indispensible guide to the roses we buy and grow: the *ARS Handbook for Selecting Roses*. It rates each rose listed on a scale of 1 to 10.

Another bonus is that all roses are listed by their official designations and classes, so you know exactly which cultivar, species or variety you're looking up when you're deciding whether to grow it in your garden.

Ratings change year by year as the word comes in about how particular varieties are doing in our gardens.

If you're serious about growing and enjoying roses, consider joining the ARS. For more information, write them at:

American Rose Society
8877 Jefferson Paige Road
Shreveport, LA 71119-8817

or phone
(318) 938-5402

or fax
(318) 938-5405

The ARS also maintains a Web site: www.ars.org

All America Rose Selections (AARS) Web Site

The Rose Resource, at www.rose.org, is the Web site of the AARS, which since 1938 has awarded the AARS medal to signify the best new rose varieties coming onto the American market.

Mail-order Rose Suppliers

Almost all large mail-order nurseries carry roses in their widely distributed catalogs. Here are some of the rose growers and suppliers who make roses their specialty:

Antique Rose Emporium
Rt. 5, Box 143
Brenham, TX 77830

Blossoms & Bloomers
11415 East Krueger Ln.
Spokane, WA 99207

The public chooses "Portland's Best Rose" each year during the Portland Rose Festival.

Portland, Oregon has one of the finest public rose gardens in the world in Washington Park.

Bridges Roses
2734 Toney Road
Lawndale, NC 28090

Butner's Old Mill Nursery
806 S. Belt Hwy.
St. Joseph, MO 64507

Edmunds' Roses
6235 SW Kahle Rd.
Wilsonville, OR 97070

Forestfarm
990 Tetherow Rd.
Williams, OR 97544-9599

Giles Ramblin' Roses
2968 State Road 710
Okeechobee, FL 34974

Greenmantle Nursery
3010 Ettersburg Rd.
Garberville, CA 95542

Heirloom Old Garden Roses
24062 Riverside Dr. NE
St. Paul, OR 97137

High Country Roses
P.O. Box 148
Jensen, UT 84035

Historical Roses
1657 W. Jackson St.
Painesville, OH 44077

Hortico, Inc.
723 Robson Rd., RR 1
Waterdown, Ontario
Canada L0R 2H1

Jackson & Perkins Co.
One Rose Lane
Medford, OR 97501-0702

Lowe's Own Root Roses
6 Sheffield Rd.
Nashua, NH 03062

Pickering Nurseries, Inc.
670 Kingston Rd.
Pickering, Ontario
Canada L1V 1A6

The Roseraie at Bayfields
P.O. Box R
Waldoboro, ME 04572

The Rose Ranch
P.O. Box 10087
Salinas, CA 93912

Roses Unlimited
Rt. 1, Box 587
Laurens, SC 29360

Sequoia Nursery
Moore Miniature Roses
2519 E. Noble Ave.
Visalia, CA 93292

Vintage Gardens
3003 Pleasant Hill Rd.
Sebastopol, CA 95472

ROSES ACROSS AMERICA

From Roseburg, Oregon to Roseville, Ohio, hundreds of towns and villages have been named after the rose. A grand tour of rose sites in the United States would take us through Rosepine, Louisiana; Rose Valley, Pennsylvania; Rosebud, South Dakota (south and east of Rosebud County, Montana); and Rose City, Texas.

We could also go to Santa Rosa, California, on our way to find Citizen Kane's "Rosebud" sled at San Simeon. We'd motor through several different Rosedales, including one in Indiana and one in Maryland. We could visit the Rosedale district of Kansas City, Kansas, on our way to the Kansas town of Rose Hill. That name's so popular that when we head to Virginia, we'd find two different towns named Rose Hill.

But no rose odyssey would be complete without a visit to Wild Rose, Wisconsin (pop. 676). If I ever hear of a rose-flavored cheese, I'd head there to find some.

Wayside Gardens
1 Garden Way
Hodges, SC 29695-0001

Specialists in Miniature Roses

Justice Miniature Roses
5947 SW Kahle Rd.
Wilsonville, OR 97070

Nor'East Miniature Roses
P.O. Box 307
Rowley, MA 01969

Oregon Miniature Roses
8285 SW 185th Ave.
Beaverton, OR 97077-5742

Pixie Treasures
4121 Prospect Ave.
Yorba Linda, CA 92686

Rose Gardens

The U.S. boasts some of the finest public rose gardens in the world. These are worth a special trip if you love roses. Most towns and cities have their own special rose gardens too. Visit these gardens to see how roses do in your particular area. And talk shop with the rosarians!

Alabama
Bellingrath Gardens, Theodore

Arkansas
State Capitol Rose Garden, Little Rock

California
Descanso Gardens, La Cañada Flintridge
Filoli Center, Woodside
Huntington Botanical Gardens, San Marino
Pageant of Roses Garden, Whittier
Tournament of Roses Wrigley Garden, Pasadena

Colorado
War Memorial Rose Garden, Littleton

Fuller Gardens in New Hampshire is a gem of a formal rose garden, set right next to the ocean.

Delaware
Hagley Museum and Library, Wilmington

District of Columbia
The United States Botanic Garden

Florida
Florida Cypress Gardens, Cypress Gardens

Georgia
Atlanta Botanical Garden, Atlanta

Idaho
Julia Davis Memorial Rose Garden, Boise

Iowa
Vander Veer Park Municipal Rose Garden, Davenport

Illinois
Chicago Botanic Garden, Glencoe
Washington Park Botanical Garden, Springfield

Kansas
Reinisch Rose Garden (Gage Park), Topeka

Louisiana
American Rose Center (ARS headquarters), Shreveport
Hodges Gardens, Many

Massachusetts
Kelleher Rose Garden, Boston
Arnold Arboretum, Jamaica Plain
Old Sturbridge Village, Sturbridge

Michigan
Frances Park Memorial Garden, Lansing

Minnesota
Lyndale Park Municipal Rose Garden, Minneapolis
Minnesota Landscape Arboretum, Chanhassen

Missouri
Laura Conyers Smith Municipal Rose Garden (Loose Park), Kansas City
Missouri Botanic Gardens, St. Louis

Nevada
Municipal Rose Garden, Reno

New Hampshire
Fuller Gardens, North Hampton

New Jersey
van der Groot Rose Garden (Colonial Park), East Millstone

New York
Brooklyn Botanical Garden, Brooklyn
New York Botanical Garden, Bronx
Old Westbury Gardens, Old Westbury
Central Park Rose Gardens, Schenectady

North Carolina
Biltmore Estate, Asheville

North Dakota
International Peace Garden, Dunseith

Ohio
Columbus Park of Roses, Columbus

Oregon
International Rose Test Garden (Washington Park), Portland

Pennsylvania
Longwood Gardens, Kennett Square
Morris Arboretum, Philadelphia
Robert Pyle Memorial Rose Gardens, West Grove

South Carolina
Edisto Memorial Gardens, Orangeburg

Tennessee
Memphis Municipal Rose Garden, Memphis

Texas
Fort Worth Botanic Garden, Fort Worth
Municipal Rose Garden, Tyler

Virginia
Norfolk Botanical Garden, Norfolk

Wisconsin
Olbrich Gardens, Madison

For more information: The Rose Resource, www.rose.org, lists the 137 AARS public test gardens by state.

ROSES TO THE RESCUE

Quick: What do roses and canaries have in common?

Yes, canaries are yellow and some roses are too, but that's not what I had in mind.

While covering the Portland Rose Festival, I visited several rose growers in Oregon's Willamette Valley. Everything seems to grow there: roses, nut crops, berries galore; horses, sheep, llamas, and dairy cows; sod farms, mint and herbs. And grapes! There must be 25 vineyards within two hours of Portland.

I pulled in to Ponzi Vineyards late one afternoon, to drink in the scenery and sample the fruit of the vine. I began to take photos of the rows and rows of vines that run seemingly for miles, set in a stunning valley amid tall, stately trees. As I did, I noticed some big, sprawling Hybrid Teas planted at the end of each row.

They didn't seem meticulously groomed, so I asked about them in the tasting house. "Oh, those. Yes, we keep them there to warn us about the crops," said a couple of Ponzi employees over a glass of late-harvest Riesling.

What exactly about the crops, I asked. Well, grapevines are subject to mildew, they reminded me; especially grapes grown in damp climates. Long ago, winemakers discovered that some kinds of roses get mildew even sooner than grapes do. So they plant rose bushes near the vines—if the roses begin to get mildew, they know that it's time to spray the grapes.

Where do the canaries come in? For decades, miners used caged canaries to tell them when the air was getting thin down below. When the canaries stopped singing, they knew to get out of the mines, and quick. Winemakers use roses in the same way, as harbingers of impending peril.

Canaries and roses. As if being beautiful weren't enough, they can sing out danger too.

GLOSSARY

acid soil n. Soil with a pH of less than 7.0. Most roses do best in soils with a pH of 6.5 to 6.8. Also called "sour" soil. *See* pH factor.

alba adj. Latin for white.

alkaline soil n. Soil with a pH of 7.1 or higher. Also called "sweet" or "basic" soil. *See* pH factor.

arch n. A supporting structure for climbing roses or other vines or upright plants that forms an opening or passageway.

balled adj. Of a flower bud that rots or fails to open properly.

bare-root rose n. One bought or shipped without soil.

bower n. An arch-shaped trellis, usually with latticework, for supporting roses.

bud n. A swelling that contains undeveloped or unopened leaves or flowers.

budding n. A propagation method of grafting a leaf bud onto rootstock.

bud union n. The part of a grafted rose where the understock meets the bud, out of which forms the top growth, a swollen

"knob" generally a few inches above the roots.

bush n. A small or neatly trained shrub.

calyx n. The green cover of the flower bud, formed from the sepals, which protects the bud.

cane n. A basal shoot or main stem.

class n. A designation by the American Rose Society to organize roses by their types: Damask, Hybrid Tea, Rambler et al. A recent *Handbook for Selecting Roses* listed 40 classes.

compost n. Material rich in nutrients, the result of decomposed organic matter. Used as a soil amendment or mulch. v. To convert something to compost.

crown n. The area where the canes or stems sprout from the bud union.

cultivar n. A contraction of "cultivated variety" of a plant. Abbr.: cv. Cultivars retain their characteristics when propagated. Roses boast of over 20,000 cultivars.

deadhead v. To remove flower heads or spent flowers.

dieback n. The dying of plant tips or shoots from climate or disease.

disbud v. To remove buds to promote production of larger or better-quality blooms.

division n. A propagation method that involves dividing a dormant plant into separate parts.

dormant adj. Describes a plant that has temporarily stopped growth, usually in winter.

family n. A group of related genera. Roses are of the family *Rosaceae*.

flush n. A bloom period.

genus (pl. genera) n. A group of plants with common characteristics. Designated with italics and a capital letter: *Rosa* is the genus of the roses.

graft union n. The point where top growth has been grafted onto the rootstock.

grafting n. A propagation method where one plant is created by uniting a shoot or bud with a rootstock of two different plants.

groundcover n., adj. A low-growing rose; often one that spreads well.

hardiness n. The ability of a plant to survive freezing temperatures outside. *See* Zone.

hardpan n. A subsoil layer so compacted that it impedes or prevents root penetration.

heat-zone system n. A rating based on the number of days with temperatures over 86°F, when heat stress begins to affect plants.

heel in v. To plant in a temporary location.

hip n. The fruit of the rose, a seedpod that turns shades of red when ripe. Many roses' hips are high in vitamin C and are eaten by birds and, in some forms, by people.

hybrid n. The result of a cross between two different species or varieties.

lateral cane n. A side branch of a main cane.

leaf node n. The point where a cane or stem bears a leaf bud or leaf.

lutea adj. Latin for yellow.

Malmaison, la n. The Empress Josephine's garden estate near Paris, where she aggressively collected and grew roses and many other plants.

neutral soil n. Soil with a pH of 7.0. *See* pH factor.

non-remontant adj. Blooming once in a growing season.

own-root adj. Grown from cuttings; a rose not budded onto another stock.

patented adj. Rose varieties or cultivars protected by govern-

Miniature 'Starina'.

ment patent. U.S. plant patents last for 17 years and serve to guarantee that the rose you buy is true to name.

perennial n, adj. A plant that lives in outdoor conditions for more than two years. Roses are perennials.

pergola n. A structure of pillars and crosspieces used to create a walkway covered by trained roses.

perpetual-flowering adj. Synonym of remontant.

petal n. The showy part of the flower within the sepals.

pH factor n. A measure of a soil's acidity or alkalinity based on hydrogen ions. Most roses prefer a pH of 6.5-6.8. *See also* acidic soil, alkaline soil, neutral soil.

PPAF adj. Plant Patent Applied For, an official designation of U.S. patent status.

prickle n. Officially, the sharp protective points on a rose. "Thorn" is a more commonly used term.

pruning n. Selectively cutting a plant for better health, production, and/or shape.

quartered adj. A petal form where the center petals are folded into four quarters. One example is 'Souvenir de la Malmaison'.

recurrent adj. Synonym of repeat-flowering.

Redouté, Pierre-Joseph (1759-1840). Painter of plants, especially Josephine's collections at la Malmaison, whose works include the exquisite *Les Roses*.

remontant adj. Flowering more than once during a growing season, whether continually or intermittently.

repeat-flowering adj. Flowering again after the first or main blooming flush.

rootstock n. The understock or host plant used for grafting a bud or scion.

Rosa n. The genus of the rose. It contains more than 100 species.

Rosaceae n. The rose family, containing over 100 genera (including those of cherries, plums, pears, apples, hawthorns and serviceberries) and 3,000 species.

rosarian n. A grower or fancier of roses; a rose expert.

rosary n. Once any place where roses were grown; now a form of devotion based on a string of "rosary" beads. From the Latin for rose garden.

rose n. The common name for *Rosa*.

rose arch: n. *See* arch

rose bower: n. *See* bower

rose hip: n. *See* hip.

rose tree n. A standard rose, one trained and pruned to grow on a single trunk.

rosery n. Any place where cultivated roses are grown, including a nursery of roses or a rosary.

rosetum n. A garden or section of one (e.g. a border) that concentrates on the cultivation of roses.

rugose adj. Wrinkled, as the leaves of *Rosa rugosa*.

scion n. A bud or shoot used in grafting to a rootstock.

sepal n. Part of the protective calyx surrounding the petals, sometimes showy.

shoot n. A stem or cane.

shrub n, adj. 1) A class of versatile, tough roses that can be used for hedges, groundcovers, mixed with others in borders, etc. 2) Any plant with woody and multiple stems. All roses are shrubs in this sense.

species n. Plants that share distinctive essential features—leaf shape, flower color—and breed true. Species roses serve several gardening purposes besides providing vital breeding stock.

specimen plant n. One grown or placed to accent its features as an individual plant, as opposed to its role in a group.

sport n. A natural change in a plant's genetic makeup, for example, a bush-form plant that suddenly becomes a climber.

Miniature 'Puppy Love'.

standard n. Any plant trained and shaped to grow on one trunk.

stock: n. *see* rootstock.

sucker n. A stem or shoot that rises from rootstock below the bud union.

thorn n. A sharp spine or prickle on a rose stem that protects the plant from predators (and reminds the gardener to be careful).

tilth n. General condition or quality of a soil, used for soil as "health" is used for living organisms.

tree rose n. Synonym for standard.

understock n. The rose that gives the rootstock for grafting.

variety n. (abbr.: var.) Generally, any distinct form of a species or hybrid. Technically, a variant of a species in the wild that breeds true. *See* cultivar.

winterize v. To protect from the cold.

winter-kill n. Death of plant cells or plants due to winter conditions.

zone n. A designation for an area with similar hardiness conditions. Roses and other perennials are rated by a system of hardiness zones; for example, a Zone 4 rose will tolerate winter conditions between -20° and -30°F.

GENERAL INDEX

INDEX OF ROSES